THE WATCHER AND THE RED DEER

THE WATCHER AND
THE RED DEER

BY

RICHARD PERRY

DAVID & CHARLES : NEWTON ABBOT

ISBN 0 7153 5385 3

First published 1952, William Hodge & Company Limited
New impression 1971

Set in Baskerville
and printed in Great Britain
by Redwood Press Limited Trowbridge
for David & Charles (Publishers) Limited
South Devon House Newton Abbot Devon

For Richard Jr. who approved

CONTENTS

I

AUTUMN

A WESTERLY gale lashed the mountains, driving torrential rain horizontally, even upwards, through a deep ravine in the heart of the hills. Laden clouds sank lower and lower, fringing 3,000-feet crests, then entombing the hills and filling the glen with swirling mists of dank grey-white vapour.

To the watcher, crouching in the lee of a granite block, glacier poised on the steep face of one hill, life was elemental, composed of wind's fury, hissing rain and the dull roar of a thousand creamy burns in spate, cascading down precipitous slopes and gouging chasms through beds of grey scree, in their fall to the rocky gorge of this wild canyon.

And then there was a new sound in the glen, not heard there, or anywhere on the hills, this past summer or spring or winter: though at this season of autumn glens and corries had reverberated to it every year for unknown thousands of years—long before men had hacked and burnt their way up the strath rivers, through the endless forests of oak, birch and pine that covered all the Highlands of Scotland to a height of 2,000 feet; and higher, clinging to naked screes on mountain sides, and marching up glens and ravines to the vast uplands lying at 3,000 feet on the roof of the Highlands.

Higher than that they could not live, for the pitiless winds that swept the mountain tundras. Only the pygmies of their kind could survive up there in the clouds: the dwarf willows, whose strength lay in thick tap-roots, driving down through gravel and frost-split rock from wiry blue-green mats of foliage. Their proud stature was measured in millimetres rather than in inches.

From out the dense concealing mists, then, there came to the watcher in the ravine a deep moaning sound, as of the wind booming through the crag-bound gorge. And, when the scudding wind tore a rift in the clouds enveloping the sharp curving ridge on the far side of the narrow gorge, into the rift paced a broad-antlered *Stag*, majestic, menacing.

Advancing to the extreme end of the ridge, he halted, and raising his head, so that antlers were laid back along his spine, roared his challenge, bass and resonant as a lion's cough, across the deep cleft of a waterfall to another stag, facing him defiant on the crest of the next great hill.

And then the two antagonists were caught up in the clouds once more—but not before this vision had been revealed to the watcher of the drama that was being enacted, this October day, on all the hills of Scotland where the wild Red Deer roamed, from the Atlantic forests of Jura and Harris in the west, eastwards to the mountain massifs of the Grampians and Easter Ross, and almost to the shores of the North Sea in far Caithness.

For this was the season of the Rut, the mating time of the red deer, which brought with it this recurring marvel of new utterance. In all the high places, in glens and corries, was to be heard this wailing and snarling, this lowing and caterwauling of the red stags. Yet for eleven months past the stags had been virtually dumb, giving vent at most to an occasional low grunt or bark: but now, with the impelling urge to mate, was reborn the gift of tongue and with it the most impressive voice of the hills—this menacing, blood-curdling roar, causing the hairs to creep on the nape of a man's neck when, lying out in the moonlight in the frosty glen, he was suddenly assailed by this almost tortured bellowing.

*   *   *   *   *

When, later in the afternoon, the clouds began to lift off the hill crests the watcher saw that all along the steep slopes on either side the ravine were deer, feeding—upwards of 300 all told, marshalled in ten or twelve herds, of which the largest numbered some sixty hinds and younger followers.

Prominent among the hinds were those that were yeld, without calves. Sleek with a summer's grazing on the abundant sedges and sparser grasses of the high pastures and corries, their rich red-brown hides stood out against green slopes in marked contrast to the dun-yellow or dark-brown milk-hinds, who had suckled calves since June, and perhaps a yearling, too, for most of twelve months before that.

But so perfectly did these vari-coloured reddish or dun-coloured deer blend with their background of brown or dull green heather that it was well-nigh impossible, on this grey day, to pick them up immediately with the naked eye at a distance of more than 400 or 500 yards; and some herds the watcher located only after prolonged scrutiny through his glass, aided by an occasional roar from the stags accompanying them.

For two or three big stags were grazing, fitfully and
restlessly, with each of the larger herds.   Among
these eight or nine big fellows was one with a broken
leg, who would not come into rut this autumn, and
two hummels without antlers.   These hummels,
who had been antlerless from birth, were strong
beasts, their strength the greater in that none had
been sacrificed to achieving those magnificent emblems
adorning most male red deer.

But as yet it was only the second day of October,
and the weather unfavourable.   The Rut had hardly
broken.   These stags were not active.   They roared
only sporadically and half-heartedly; and though
two big fellows, accompanying a herd of ten hinds,
might put their heads down, stretch out their back
legs, and spar with swift ripostes of antler tips,
playfully rather than in rivalry, shoving hard for
several minutes, no more would come of such fencing
but that in the end they couched down quietly a little
distance apart.

             *   *   *   *   *

Ten days later, on a fair day with a cool north
wind after the rains, the watcher came again to this
lonely glen, ten miles from the nearest settlement of
men and 1,500 feet above sea-level, to find himself
in a changed world, with the rut at the peak of its
activity.

Every hill crest, every corrie held its stag or three
or four stags, and their roaring was continuous.   Over
a square mile of the glen and the long slopes of its
empounding hills—those immense ice-flattened pyra-
mids and "slag-tips", which shelved so steeply that a

man had to throw back his head to reach their summits—he counted nineteen stags.

So strenuous was the competition for hinds that not one of these stags had succeeded in collecting, or at any rate retaining, a harem of more than fourteen hinds and followers. Some had no more than five or six hinds, and there were several wandering stags who had not yet won for themselves a single hind.

It was these wandering bachelors who incited much of the roaring. Pacing along the ridges, roaring intermittently, or couched on the skyline, their visible or audible presence kept those stags with harems in a constant state of tension.

Their un-ease was exemplified by that dark-red twelve-pointer Royal with eight hinds, most of whose hours were passed standing sentinel, a little above the watcher, on one or another of the prominent crags and heather knolls breaking up the steep slope to the ravine.

For ten years, twelve perhaps, his splendid black antlers, which branched almost at right-angles from the crown before their upward and inward curve, had grown more massive each summer, though the number of tines they carried might not have increased since he had come of age when six years old.

Now he was in his prime. With an antler beam of three feet, and shaggy mane of long coarse hair, stained black with peat, accentuating the formidable girth of swollen neck, he presented a ferocious front to any rival.

His ferociousness was increased when, stretching out his head and rounding his muzzle into an O, he roared open-mouthed, emitting an impressive volume of sound that terminated in a series of coughing grunts. And this he might do at intervals of less than a minute, and to all points of the compass.

But from time to time he would lower his head and make a pretence of nibbling a few bites of moss, or trot down from his roaring place to chivy a hind who was straying too far from the remainder of his harem. Once, he ran down to a rowan tree, leaning out over the gorge, and getting its slender bole between his antlers proceeded to work off some of his excess of energy by threshing them vigorously up and down; then trotted restlessly up to another vantage point, to bell his challenge again; whereupon a hind climbed up to his special crag: there, with long ears pricked, to survey at leisure the scene of high activity in the glen.

Long and dished of face she was, and long and lean was her ewe-neck.

And what she saw was that ever and again some other stag would suddenly trot away from his harem —not with his usual high-stepping gait, but at a smooth menacing run, with legs hardly flexed—and advance roaring up the face of the ravine a little distance, to challenge a wanderer high above him. Then he would turn about hastily and go running back to his hinds again.

There would be good reason for his apprehension; for often, when one of these master stags left his harem in this way, another stag would come charging down on the hinds from some other height. Then, cutting out a hind and her calf, feeding a little apart from the harem, the ravisher would drive them before him across the siding, with the master in hot pursuit. And now the latter's roaring would be broken by his uneasy galloping motion into a jerky succession of deep grunts—that punctuated expression of anger and frustration the watcher had heard so often in the forest on frosty, moon-bright nights. After a chase of a few hundred yards, however, the master would suddenly remember his unguarded harem, who had continued to graze unconcernedly the while; and, cutting his losses, would trot back to them, still roaring, outstretched head held low.

But, more often, a would-be ravisher beat a retreat immediately a master charged down upon him, though less precipitately when the latter advanced in his direction only slowly, with menacing caterwauling; and if a small bachelor stag, his glossy red coat still unstained by the dark brown peat of the wallows, in which most of the masters cooled their heated bodies, sat quietly on the hillside near a harem, the Lord of the harem would ignore his presence: though as soon as the bachelor rose, with ears pricked, to make his way up the hill, attracted by the roaring of another wanderer on the skyline, the master would see him off with a series of roars.

It had been early in September, a week or two before the Rut, that the master stags had opened up their autumn wallows, churning up peat-hags with their forefeet into viscous packs of liquid mud. These might be fifteen feet across and deep enough in which to roll at full stretch, or perhaps just a peat sump, half full of water, at the end of a bog-drain— a tight fit for any stag, this shapeless pan, no more than five feet by three feet; but, as the black mud slopped thickly over its shallow banks revealed, well patronised. In either case the wallow would be visited by a number of stags during the course of the day, but especially in the early morning when the sun was warming up, and again in the evening before feeding.

Rivalry among the stags was not, however, restricted to masters *versus* wanderers. Two masters, one with eleven hinds, and the other, another red stag, with only five, were in possession of harems only 200 or 300 yards apart, low down on the siding across the ravine immediately opposite the watcher. These two, to his amusement, roared continuously, as they advanced and retreated intermittently towards and away from a hind and her calf, who were grazing in a no-stag's land midway between the two harems. But after each initial advance of a few score yards from their respective harems, neither master would adventure closer to the errant hind, and would stand roaring impotently at one another, on either side of that invisible barrier of mutual respect—they were much of a size—which held them back from the prize; or would walk parallel with one another, thirty or forty yards apart, bellowing and tossing their antlers; before in the end, one or other would turn about and stalk slowly back to his harem.

That their sense of frustration was very real, yet subordinate to their acute judgment of their opponent's physical strength, was illustrated by the red stag, who, after returning to his harem from one of these sorties, spent several minutes releasing his pent-up anger in tearing up the heather viciously with the point of his antlers, tossing stems and clods over his back.

Such was usually the procedure when either stag was already in possession of a harem. But only a few hundred yards further up the ravine two more stags, of whom the lighter beast was a bachelor, had not sized up each other's armaments so precisely, and were swaying backwards and forwards, antlers locked, in a vigorous shoving match, with heads bowed and turned back a little to one side and mane-thickened necks arched. First one, and then the other, would gather his hind legs well under his belly and give a tremendous heave, in herculean, but vain, attempt to throw his opponent. Round and round they scrimmaged, antlers still locked, clods of peat and turf flying up from champing hooves. Then, breaking apart, one thrust with lightning stroke at unguarded flank; but was foiled by equally swift parry with antlers.

Four such savage and prolonged engagements, and they drew apart a few paces for a breathing space, hollow flanks heaving. Gone were the fat paunches of August, but the dynamic strength contained in those powerful shoulders and cut-away hindquarters had to be seen to be believed, and was most spectacularly demonstrated by that *one*-antlered stag who threw a Royal, as heavy as himself, a complete somersault— demonstrated, too, the resilience of that one antler, weighing no more than two or three pounds, that could bear the strain of a weight nearly one hundred times its own. That this hero bolted, before the no doubt bewildered Royal could get to his feet, did not lessen the majesty of his achievement!

The master of the harem had the tactical advantage of being uphill of his challenger, and this, coupled with his superior weight, soon began to tell in his favour. Twenty yards at a time he would push the other back with furious battling runs, and after a few more minutes the challenger, disentangling his antlers, wheeled around and retreated downhill at the double—though not before he had suffered a savage jab in the ribs from the master's antlers.

Victory achieved, the master roared several times. Then, pacing to a boggy place, he rolled, by way of cooling off: finally digging his antlers into the bog and tossing wet peat over his back.

But lesser stags must rest, and when in the grey evening the watcher came down out of that deep canyon on to the broad grassy flat of the main glen, he passed a small red stag couched peacefully high up on the hill face. Eyes closed, he was apparently unaware of the sound and fury all around him, while his harem of six or seven hinds, grazing close at hand, had not been sighted by the ubiquitous bachelors, who were still travelling the dizzy heights above.

*   *   *   *   *

It was now the season of the Merry Dancers. Their ghostly shimmering veils flickered restlessly to and fro across the night sky; and their northern messengers, the wild swans, forging south from Iceland in wedge-shaped squadrons, charmed the watcher to his open window with their far-off bugle-notes.

The swans brought with them a grey dusting of snow to the high tops; but it was Indian Summer, with a hot sun shining from an hour after sunrise until sunset, and all the moors glistening with the frost-spangled webs of countless myriads of spiders, when the watcher again visited the rutting glen only two days after he had found it a scene of furious action.

But now the glen had been mysteriously evacuated by the deer. The fine weather had drawn them up to the tops, where on previous days he had glimpsed, from the depths of the glen, the tiny figures of wanderers on the crests, and had thrilled to that first vision of the two masters challenging from the clouds. Now he was perforce to enter the deer's own world on the high uplands.

So it was that by noon he had climbed more than a thousand feet up the stalker's pony-path, a rough track of water-scoured gravel and rock, that zigzagged in sharp diagonals up the almost sheer, and in places overhanging, face of that great hill whose enormous bulk loomed above the long U-shaped glacial loch at the entrance to the glen.

On breasting the 2,750-foot summit he had found himself face to face with an ivory-tined, beige-maned stag of seven points, who was couched peacefully in the noonday sun with his harem of six grey-necked hinds around him.

Their resting place was a flat of white rock chips, sparsely carpeted with patches of dwarf heather, still a fresh green at this altitude, though tinted reddish-brown at their tips; with soft drab-coloured fringe-moss and false reindeer-moss, whose brittle ash-white filigree-work resembled miniature antlers; and with the silvery-backed palmate leaves of the creeping lady's-mantle.

Regretting his unwary approach through this gateway to the deer's world, the watcher sank down

on the rough heather to cool his sweaty body in the
light northerly air, fresh as spring water, which
played over the summit plateau.

On this brilliantly clear day, with the blue-white
heaven cloudless except for a few wisps of wind-
carded cirrus, the most distant ranges of mountains
were faultlessly defined. North, east, south and west
tawny mountain tablelands stretched away and
away to higher blue-black, cone-shaped peaks and
long whale-backs; and all the 400 square miles
within his ken—and far beyond—was deer country.

Northwards, ten miles down the riverside track
through moor and glen, his house was hidden in the
pinewoods. Lying a thousand feet above sea-level,
between steeply rising moors on the one side, and
birchen dells skirting loch and water-meadows in
the broad strath on the other, it was ringed round
by mountains of red deer, eight miles from pine-
forested base to base. Were he not out in the glens
or on the hills, he yet had the deer within range of
his glass—and the roe deer on his doorstep: for that
morning a doe and her two fawns had still been
nibbling at the turnips in his field, when a warm sun
was just rising over the hills.

The deer were to him what their flocks and herds
were to those of his neighbours who did not regard
their stock solely as gold on the hoof. That the deer
were wild increased rather than detracted from the
pleasure of his relationship with them. The need to
approach them gently and with circumspection
rendered this relationship the more fascinating, for
its full achievement was a challenge not only to his
physical endurance but to his field-craft—to his

powers of observation and deduction, and to his sympathetic insight into deer mentality.

There was, moreover, the deep satisfaction of knowing every inch of his country: those 250,000 acres of desolate mountain ridges and windswept uplands, those boundless heaths and moors, those dark pine forests and green glens of birch and alder; of elucidating their light and shade, their cairns and hollows; of appraising the endless pursuit of clouds across the sky, not always chasing the same course as the fickle winds in the corries. In his study of the deer, the flight of birds was significant, as were the rippling swathes of innumerable grass-stems.

Those bare reddish tors and grey cones, fifteen miles eastward as the raven flew over hill and moor and corrie, were the highest portions of the mountain barrier ringing a vast upland. On its rough pastures hundreds of stags summered. Among them were some he had watched in the rutting glen. They had been attracted to this forest by the 600 or 700 hinds whose winter home it was. Other stags had come in still further from the mountain corries and glens beyond that upland.

The distant lowing and wailing of stags was indeed the only sound in the hills this October noon, other than the eternal roar and fall of tumbling burns and, once, the deep croak of a raven; as, wrapping sable wings around taughtened body, he allowed himself to fall, "wingless," for fifty feet, rolling over on his back as he did so, before righting himself, with silken lash of unfurling wings, and continuing his direct flight high above the dark blue waters of the loch: from whose sandy surround, contoured by alternate

drought and spate, a bronze canopy of birches
billowed up steep, flood-scarred screes which had
fallen from the long serrated frieze of black crags above.

The marshy green floor of the glen below was
seamed and veined by the straight furrows of old
drainage channels, cut, providently, by the shieling
folk, who had summer-pastured their flocks and herds
in this high glen a century before the watcher's day.
Serpentine coils of a peat-brown river meandered
through the glen from its fount in a "black" loch in
the upper south-west fork of the glen—a black loch
with pools of silver and the sun's shimmer dancing
over its surface.

South-eastwards that deep rutting-canyon writhed
far up into the giant hills, out of which had been
carven, gouged and eroded by glacier and river,
wind and forest, all these fearful ravines and immense
punchbowl corries. So deep were the ravines that
the midsummer sun had already left them an hour or
two after noon, shortly after first lighting them.

The black shadow of an eagle swept smoothly
across the long green sweep of a sunlit hill on the
opposite side of the glen. In July the watcher had
climbed up to her eyrie at the head of the corrie on
his right hand—one of five she used from year to year
—though rather than an eyrie it had proved to be a
comfortable couch, a broad shelf, seven feet long and
three feet wide, at the base of a rock slab. Though
commanding a wide field of vision over the main
glen, the eyrie was invisible from below, and only
the secretive departure-flight of the old eagle had
betrayed its whereabouts to him. The eaglets, for
there were two, had been almost ready to fly, and

when he clambered down to stand beside them on the ledge, the larger, two or three times the size of its fellow, had curved its great wings as if exploring the possibilities of flight, but contented itself with jumping down on to a lower ledge. He had found it difficult to credit that this magnificent dark brown, red-maned eagle was the sister of that wretched little poult, which was too feeble even to stand upright on its nest of heather stems and sheep's wool, garnished with the raw remains of rabbits. Starved by its stronger nest-fellow it would be dead by now.

*   *   *   *   *

The watcher's seat was high enough for him to overlook the lower portion of that extensive plateau sloping back indefinitely from the mountain barrier on the far side of the glen, and with his glass he could discern nine harems of deer on those tops. Scattered widely among them were many small lots of mountain sheep, of that hardy blackface breed, of which tens of thousands had been drafted into the Highlands during the past one hundred years and more: to share the deer's summer pastures up to a height of 3,000 feet, and to rob them of their winter grazing in the glens of birch and alder and in the park-like pine forests.

On his hill, however, there was more activity with fifteen stags, seven of them wanderers, within his field of view. But all were afar off: so he turned inwards, along the narrow divide between two punch-bowl corries, intent to explore the vast expanse of high moors that lay westwards—a wilderness of heather and peat-hags, and of bogs betrayed by the

vivid dark-green of star-moss. And it was then that
he perceived on the near skyline of a 3,000-feet tor
a herd of thirty or forty hinds, and milling around
the herd no fewer than six stags. Creeping up to a
bog-hole, he lay down to watch.

Like collies with a flock of sheep, so these six stags
were galloping round and round the hinds, without
a second's respite; while intermittently one or other
of them would attempt, unsuccessfully, to cut out
and drive off a hind or group of hinds. But though
roaring continuously, and passing and repassing so
closely that their antlers scraped, the stags were not
actively militant towards one another. On the contrary it was the hinds who were aggressive, prancing
on their hind legs and boxing at each other with
swinging forefeet: for they were kept in a state of
nerves by the constant chivying of one big stag, whose
incessant rounding-up and herding of this large
harem successfully prevented any one of the other
five stags from driving off any of the hinds.

And not only were the hinds irritable. They also
displayed every sign of fear when one of the would-be
ravishers ran at them—head held low, muzzle
rounded, lips drawn back—rearing away from him
like wild horses. Once, however, when the master
charged at a hind who was straying too far from her
fellows, she, contrarily, stood her ground. What
was more, when he was almost upon her, she calmly
lowered her head and scratched the side of her jaw.
This surprising act of cool defiance brought the stag
to a hesitant stop, and after looking at her for a few
moments he turned about and returned to the harem
at a fast trot.

This milling vortex of bellowing confusion naturally attracted the attention of all wandering stags, and also unattached hinds, within range; and after half an hour or so the watcher realized that the number of stags present had increased to nine, of which all, with one exception, were engaged in mass onslaught upon the sanctity of the harem. Nor was it until a further half-hour had elapsed that, one by one, the unsuccessful bachelors—two of them were one-antlered—began to retreat from the turmoil, slowly and reluctantly, often halting to look back.

Their breaking off the engagement was not due to any direct aggression by the master stag, who continued, without rest, to herd and chivy the hinds. These lesser stags were exhausted by their physical exertions. One or two of them, indeed, couched down in the heather, spent, while the others made a pretence of feeding, raising their heads from time to time to gaze at the hinds, even advancing a few paces towards the roaring master; but even so, when one hind did succeed in slipping away from the harem, and one of the spent stags rose to his feet and went forward to meet her, he subsequently showed no further interest in her, grazing quietly at her side. The master, for his part, though trotting after her initially, did not pursue her far—she was a young hind, by her short head—and after roaring vengefully at his usurper, turned back to join his harem.

Gradually all the bachelors grazed away from the harem, or wandered off in search of more accessible hinds, and the master was left in sole possession, with the solitary exception of one big stag, couched peacefully in the heather midway between the watcher and the harem. He had taken no part in the on-slaught, being spent no doubt from his activities before the watcher had come on the scene, and had passed much of his time roaring at the latter.

Him the master ignored, trotting off instead for a hasty roll in a small dub of water; and for a few minutes there was peace on the hill. The harassed hinds settled down to rest and cud, though the older ones among them could never relax, continually raising and depressing their long ears, and sniffing the light air, still, providentially, across the watcher's front.

But the presence at the peak of the Rut of so large and conspicuous a gathering of hinds could not fail to serve as a lodestar for all unattached stags, wandering their indeterminate ways over the hill-tops. Before long the master had his hinds on their feet once more, and rounding them up indefatigably, he herded them slowly westwards. At the same time he was still repelling the late-coming raiders and was, moreover, actually increasing his harem by going out to meet stranger hinds. The threat of his menacing roars was now, however, sufficient to frighten off these fresh stags, new hinds joining the harem without incident.

By evening the master had driven the last of his hinds over the skyline, still accompanied as rearguard by that faithful squire, of a size with himself. The latter had now begun roaring again, sporadically, in the watcher's direction, and in the cooling air the breath was blown from his nostrils in steamy jets.

Though the eastern peaks were still rose-clear in the purple after-glow of sunset, a bright moon was rising high into the paling sky, and the west was a velvety green-black, as the squire passed over the brow of the tor—the last deer of the day—and the watcher rose stiffly from his bog-hole, to make his painful way down into the cold shade of the glen, from which the mountain sheep were filing up their thin tracks to their breezy night-places high up on the grassy slopes.

*   *   *   *   *

That master of forty hinds had demonstrated what a phenomenal output of energy was demanded from such a stag in obtaining, and retaining, a large harem of hinds—though it had to be admitted that he squandered no small portion of his energy in chasing young staggies who, though harmless, seemed to arouse the ire of big stags during the Rut.

It was not usual to see a large harem of hinds in the middle of October, when the Rut was at its height. Such large harems, containing seventy or eighty hinds in some instances, were commonly seen by the watcher only late in September or early in October, before the majority of the stags had come in to the rutting glens, whence the hinds had preceded them. Such early stags, and they were likely to be the oldest and strongest, had little competition with which to contend. Likewise, large harems might sometimes be seen very late in the year, when all but a handful of stags had finished rutting.

This master had herded his hinds on to ground ideal for his purposes—flat, open and with a wide field of view. He could see far, move freely, and keep his harem under control. Those stags with harems on the precipitous faces of ravines had difficulty in keeping their hinds together on such broken ground, and never knew from what direction a rival might charge down upon the harem.

Nevertheless, the watcher knew that the master had probably not won and kept his numerous harem by actual combat. That would not only have dissipated his physical energies, but would also have been waged to little purpose, since a stag engaged in battle could not at the same time defend his harem from the incursion of any other unattached stag or stags, who might seize such a heaven-sent opportunity to steal his hinds. Moreover, by setting a premium on a stag's powers of endurance, rather than on his prowess as a fighter, Nature insured that it was these most physically perfect stags, endowed with maximum endurance, that served the greatest number of hinds. Not only could these prime stags outlast their less enduring rivals, but it was they too who, because of their ability to condition well, came into rut earliest in the autumn when the greatest proportion of hinds were available to them.

Thus those qualities of physical hardihood, most essential to the survival of the red deer in the ultra-rigorous conditions of their habitat, were perpetuated in the greatest possible number of calves.

By the middle of October competition for hinds was so strenuous that those stags with harems might have few opportunities for mating, and young stags, coming into rut late in the season, might mate with more hinds than their immediate predecessors.

Man, as usual, had done his blind best to upset Nature's admirable control, but fortunately for the deer the possession by a stag of a magnificent head of antlers—the stalker's prize—did not necessarily co-incide with the most perfect physique, any more than a blackface ram with an impressive head of curling horns could be relied upon to beget good lambs; and though the watcher had some evidence to suggest that hummels begot hummels and stags with malformed antlers, the strong hummel had his part to play in preserving the physical hardihood of the herds.

Had these not been the facts of the stag's natural history then it was the watcher's opinion that the Scottish red deer might well have degenerated ere this to a race of undersized runts, for its stags had been subjected for the past 150 years to a persistent culling of the finest heads.

*   *   *   *   *

There were, of course, occasions on which stags did fight during the rutting season, and a mighty clashing and rattling of antlers there was when they fought.

Once the watcher had lain close to two well-matched stags while they battled on a heather flat for upwards of one hour, with only the briefest rests; and at one point he had noted with amusement that even the hinds, who usually ignored stag fights, had bunched together at a safe distance to look on. So exhausted were the two antagonists towards the end of this interminable contest of lunge and thrust and parry, with antlers locked for long periods, that neither could rise from his knees; and it was mutual exhaustion and not injury that ultimately brought their struggle to an indecisive conclusion, for both appeared insensible to pain, no matter how savage the lunges of the other.

But the fiercest engagement of which the watcher had been an awed witness had been short and sharp when, with much menacing pawing of the ground and tossing of antlers, an eight-pointer and a ten-pointer had gradually backed away from each other to fifty or sixty yards, and then had charged hell-for-leather, as he had seen two doughty blackface rams do, to collide with a thunderous crash, whose fearful impact drove both stags back upon their haunches. And that had been sufficient unto the day thereof for both half-stunned contestants, whose skulls, tough as they might be, were not unbreakable.

Such fierce or prolonged combats were not, however, characteristic of stags in rut. If two did set to in full earnest, the normal practice was for each to attempt to turn the other's antlers and gore his flank, with the almost invariable result that one made a desperate leap back and to one side at the critical instant, avoiding injury. Not one stag in 200 was killed by another stag.

The watcher had heard that clashing of bony antlers in the night more often than by day. In the darkness, perhaps, a stag was unable to assess the strength of a rival, except by trial of combat; and it was certainly at night, when bachelor stags enjoyed the most favourable opportunities for raiding the harems, and when most of those masters of harems mated with their hinds, that the rutting glens were most full of sound and fury. But, in a typical engagement by day, the lighter or less formidably antlered

stag usually sought to break away as soon as he
became aware of his rival's superiority in weight or
armament; while two well-matched stags might even
walk peaceably apart, after having had their antlers
locked for several minutes; and it had always mystified
the watcher that so few instances had been recorded
of those intricately tined antlers becoming inextricably
entangled in combat—till death did them part. In
more vigorous break-aways, however, he had known
cases of an antler being broken off or of a mortal
wound inflicted by a chance lunge in such a vital
spot as the jugular vein.

There was no gainsaying that stags were savage
beasts while in rut, though mild enough at other
seasons, and a wandering stag would tilt savagely
at any small, or sick stag unable to escape his on-
slaught, bowling him over with a single vicious
lunge of his antlers, and then perhaps jumping on
him vindictively. But such merciless incidents were
not included in Nature's plan for the perpetuation
of the red deer. They served a purpose in ridding
the forest—always overstocked in winter—of weak
and sickly male stock, and in abetting the survival of
the fittest—no more.

There was a bottom, however, to the reserves of
energy of even so physically perfect an animal as a
stag. True, for five months before the Rut the stags
had been accumulating energy, grazing peacefully
on the upland pastures and in the high corries. Even
so, summer in the mountains was more often than
not a season of heavy rains and cold winds, which
drove the deer off the tops and down to less peaceful
places.

And, before the summer came, they had suffered that desperate struggle against starvation of the Highland winter—six or seven months in a bad season, during which their main source of food, mosses and lichens, coarse sedges and young heather, might have lain buried beneath an iron-hard crust of frozen snow for weeks at a time: for two months in a hard winter. Moreover the stags began the winter in very poor condition, after the excesses of the Rut, whereas the hinds were then in better condition than they would be for another twelve-month.

It was always marvellous to the watcher that such large animals, stags averaging from twelve to seventeen stone in weight, and hinds from eight to twelve stone, could survive such conditions: reflected in the mortality rate each winter and spring of half the previous summer's stock of calves.

Their survival was the more remarkable when it was recalled that during the past 300 years the race of Scottish red deer had experienced a profound change of habitat. Before the felling and burning of the forests and, later, the coming of the sheep, the deer had lived in the immense tracts of oak and pine wood for nine months of the twelve, feeding much when grass was not in season, on the leaves and catkins of such trees and shrubs as aspens, willows, hazels and bramble. Only during the three summer months, when the mountain grazing was good, did they migrate to the high corries and uplands, where they were less troubled by insects; and even then some of the big stags might linger on the low ground in the woods until their antlers were clean of velvet in August, lying up on some small fern-covered loch island, quite near a stalker's cottage, perhaps, swimming their protective moat twice a day to their feeding place—for water was ever the friend of deer.

But now it was only during the winter storms that the deer sought shelter in pine forest and birchwood, in the few glens where such harbourage was still available to them. There were many herds of deer whose wintering glens contained no more cover than a few stunted birches straggling up the ravines, with here and there a small rowan.

Such a catastrophic change had not been countered without sacrifice. A big forest stag of the early nineteenth century might exceed thirty stone in weight and carry more than twenty points on his antlers. A big hill stag in the watcher's day did not commonly exceed seventeen stone or carry more than twelve points. Nevertheless, the red deer had adapted themselves with remarkable vigour to this change, displaying uncanny judgment in discovering shelter on open, windswept ground, to all appearances devoid of cover; and had not only maintained, but had increased their numbers, despite heavy mortality in recurring hard winters and the annual toll by stalkers of one-sixth of the stag stock and a lesser proportion of the hinds.

But without taking into account the good or bad seasons that might have preceded the Rut, no animal could continue to squander energy indefinitely at the tempo of a rutting stag, without refuelling. A week or ten days of rutting at the most, and the master stag was exhausted and also starved, pinched in the belly like a racehorse: for his constant vigilance

in guarding the harem had not allowed him leisure
to snatch more than an occasional hasty bite of
mosses and lichens and to drink heavily of peaty
water. If the rutting season was near its close, he
might remain with his hinds for a further week or
so, though allowing young stags to join the harem
and uttering no more than an occasional sleepy roar,
too lazy even to get to his feet.

More usually, however, he abandoned his hinds
at the end of his active rutting period, or was driven
from them by fresher stags, and went up to his
summer pastures if the weather was still open, or to
his traditional wintering corrie if the weather was
bad; there to regain strength before the winter
storms, consorting peaceably with other stags ful-
filling a similar mission. After a few days' rest he
might, or might not, return to the rutting glen,
travelling ten or twenty miles in one night perhaps,
for a further week or two's activity among the hinds,
after chasing off other spent stags in his turn.

*   *   *   *   *

It was a source of regret to the watcher that neither
he, nor apparently any one else, had ever witnessed
a trial of strength between two hummels. Notably
strong, the hummel was also a resourceful and
successful stag, dealing out heavy dunts with his
hard poll, which appeared to disconcert his rivals
more than did lunges from antlers. He commonly
herded a large harem during the Rut, though he
had a curious habit of voluntarily leaving his hinds
before he was spent, and wandering away. It happened exceptionally, indeed, that one stag would

chase another to such a distance that he never returned to his harem; and, again, if for any reason there was a slackening in the general rutting activity, some stags might leave their harems in the forenoon and go off on their own for a few hours' rest, returning to the hinds in the early evening.

However that might be it was also the hummel who invariably led the loosely-knit stag herd during the winter. The watcher used the term *invariably* advisedly. Hummels, both old and young, were exceptionally numerous in his forests during and after the Rut, with five full-grown beasts to every 200 antlered stags, though in most forests the ratio was one adult hummel to 100 antlered stags; and if a herd of stags included a hummel, then it was the hummel who invariably led the way in retreat, if any supposed danger threatened the herd; invariably it was the hummel who was the most suspicious or who first spotted the watcher if he were stalking.

It was, no doubt, only coincidence that this abundance of hummels was complementary to an unusual shortage of "switch-horns," those stags which when adult bore antlers clean of all points except the brow tines, and perhaps not even those. Unlike the hummel, however, a "switch" one year was capable of growing perfect antlers the next; but, like the hummel, he too was a strong, successful stag, employing the same tactics when fighting: manœuvring for a flank lunge with those long, wickedly sharp brow-points, capable of piercing to the heart of a luckless antagonist; for these were the antlered stag's killing weapons: his upper points he used for fencing and grappling.

An illuminating instance of hummel dominance
had occurred the previous winter. It had been an
exceptionally mild November, with almost perpetual
low cloud shrouding the hills in stygian gloom, so
that it was most difficult to see the deer against
the dark slopes. On the twenty-fourth day of the
month, however, had come one of those sudden cold
spells, characteristic of the mountains, with several
inches of snow on the hill and twenty degrees of
frost in the glen, and the watcher had seized the
opportunity the next day to visit the foothills below
those high uplands where the deer pastured in the
summer. Rising out of the Glen of Crags, these
forested foothills were a great stag sanctuary in
winter.

A north-westerly gale, raging all night, had left
a dusting of snow at all levels and was followed by a
brilliantly clear morning. It was one of those
mornings when, from the high moors above his house,
the watcher could just make out with the naked
eye, half an hour before noon, a small herd of stags,
only eight beasts in fact, running athwart the immense grey-white face of one foothill, though they
were three miles' distant on the hoodie's line of
flight. They looked exactly like ants, for it was
impossible to distinguish leg movement at such a
distance, except when deer were walking along a
skyline, and their antlers resembled antennæ.

Sixty or seventy more stags were feeding among the
outlying pines on a lesser hill, and a further fifty were
scraping the snow on the glinting white slope leading
to one of the 3,000-foot ridges. By noon this herd
had increased to ninety strong, as other stags climbed

up from the pine forest to join them. In all but the most prolonged snowstorms there was good feeding on the mosses and lichens on that exposed hill, for the winds swept its stony ridge clear of any depth of snow, while in fissures among the screes on its precipitous west face was a luxuriant growth of blaeberry and heather.

An hour later the watcher, having forded the river, was resting under a pine tree at the base of the hills, with the small chatter of coal and crested tits for company. At intervals a lone stag would appear on the summit of a lesser hill immediately above, and each stag would follow the same pattern of behaviour.

First, there would be a long look round, then retreat, then reappearance and another prolonged survey of the spacious glen, so peaceful on this still, calm day in the mellow light of the pale yellow wintry sun, now a little obscured by snow-cloud: glen and moors stretching away to the gleaming sweep of the rounded white fells, with their black blocks of pine-wood, flanking the western rim of the strath.

Then, at last, the decision would be made, and the stag would begin walking down the slope to the forest; but no high-spirited stag could walk downhill for long, and that crisp snow crust, smoothing out rocks and heather tumps, soon impelled him to break into a heavy bucketing canter, for the fun of the thing, antlers skirmishing with the snow.

Some would canter down towards those that had preceded them. Others struck out on their own course, with another halt for inspection, perhaps, halfway down the slope, before continuing their

descent to the blaeberry patches among the pine
trees. There, some younger stags and staggies had
been feeding all morning. Quiet studies in yellow-
browns and fawns they made, as they stood mildly
questioning the watcher, when he passed gently by
them up the old foresters' trackway to the hills.

Between the foothills and the gigantic barrier of
mountains forming the western escarpment to the
uplands was a pass, a narrow defile threaded and
studded with many small lochans in pits at the base
of steep screes. Stags passed through this Pass of the
Lochans and fed within it on almost every day of the
year from October to June; and when at three
o'clock the watcher penetrated the pass from its
lower side, it was to perceive, as he had expected,
the tail-end of what no doubt was a large herd of
stags feeding among the heather, heavily encrusted
with snow, on the opposite slope 300 yards distant.

Snow squalls were now veering from various points
behind him, and a few of the seventeen stags within
view were a little doubtful of his wind, as he lay
concealed within the banks of a frozen watercourse.
Those suspicious moved off along the pass, though
their fellows continued feeding, thrusting their long
muzzles well down into the heather.

The departure of some had not, however, passed
unnoticed, or more likely it was the retreat of a great
stag, feeding on the domed summit of a high hill
behind the watcher, that had attracted attention;
but at any rate another twenty stags came charging
down one by one over the brow of the opposite hill,
led by one of two hummels among them. They,
too, were in high spirits, and there were some brief,

but violent, collisions with antlers, a one-antlered
beast shying away from one such bout of stag-play,
while another stag pranced backwards playfully,
doing a little jig with his forefeet at the same time,
as if contemplating battle; but his inviting challenge
was not accepted.

It was only two or three weeks since these same
stags had been shot at on every hill and in every
glen. Yet to-day they allowed the watcher, a most
conspicuous object in the white glen, to walk slowly
across the snow towards them for 200 yards before
there was any movement among them.

Perhaps there was some truth after all in the
traditional belief that the red deer could distinguish
between the stalker and his rifle and the shepherd
with his dogs, between hunter and watcher. The
latter, with or without his collies, had never known
deer to panic from him except on those few occasions
when he had unwittingly come upon them abruptly.
Approaching them up-wind there was always that
long interval of contemplation, followed by leisurely
retreat to no great distance, frequently interrupted
for further inquisitive stares. Paradoxically, so long as
a man remained in full view of a herd of deer, they
displayed little fear of him, but if he raised himself
from his bog-hole and then crouched down again,
they would sometimes stampede, or at least
move off. The watcher had found that wild geese
reacted in a similar manner.

Thus, on rounding the hill into the middle of the
pass, he had all the time in the world to take a
tally of the herd scattered through the length of the
pass—105 stags in all, of all ages down to staggies

with brow points only, and including four, possibly five, big hummels.

As he walked along the pass, so the stags began to move away. Some straggled on south through the pass, following a big twelve-pointer, whose three finger-like tines on either top were bent inwards; two herds bunched up hill; while staggies, not in the least alarmed, stood indecisively in mid-pass fifty or sixty paces from him, not knowing which of their fellows to follow. A rich warm peach-brown they were, broad noses moist and black, antler tines sharp-pointed as needles. If, however, little staggies got separated from the herd, they were liable to panic, and might come to grief when the hills were deep in snow.

It was at this stage that a most significant incident occurred. One fine hummel was leading a herd of forty stags, including a massive fourteen-pointer, and breasting the almost sheer siding in the most determined manner; and as he climbed he looked round at the other stags and deliberately uttered a single guttural barking *urrk-urrk*, which, but for its slightly hoarser timbre, might have come in similar circumstances from an old hind leading her group of followers to safety. It was a genuine bark, not the pseudo moaning roar which a stag might utter at the fag-end of the rutting season; and the hummel was a mature stag, not a staggie, whom the watcher had known to bark at various seasons. He would certainly have attributed this hummel's bark to a hind, without more ado, had there been any hinds in the pass.

This incident opened up new avenues of approach to the interpretation of stag mentality. The hummel's physical state of being antlerless was clearly associated with a mental state of being more of an individualist than the antlered stag, and of having quicker or more active reactions to the external phenomena of his world. The problem was, did the other stags in a herd recognize the hummel as their leader, or did they merely follow him because he was usually the first among them to set off, without havering, in a definite direction?

Another possibility could not be entirely excluded. Was the hummel, being antlerless and of a dominant nature, mistaken for a hind by normal stags, except of course during the rutting season? For the first two or three years of their lives it was a hind whose leadership most of them had followed every day and every hour. These, at any rate, were the thoughts that passed through the watcher's mind on the long trek home, after hearing the hummel's warning bark.

*   *   *   *   *

On the day following his experience with the master stag and his forty hinds, the watcher had revisited the Eagles' Glen, but had found it difficult to believe that he was in the same forest as on those previous days of high activity. Though still summer-like, it was cooler with a stronger north-westerly breeze, and few stags could be heard roaring when this time he climbed to the east-side heights. Only one stag was to be found on that boggy tableland, a wilderness of interminably tortuous water-courses and ravines; nor could he discern much activity on the western hills, though one big stag was rolling

continually in the peat hags on one hill face. Some
of the biggest stags had only one hind apiece, and
most of the deer were making their way westwards
into the wind, as was often their habit when feeding.

Although the rutting month was barely half gone
those three days of ideal rutting weather, with their
hot summer noons and cool frosty nights, had
indeed marked the peak of an early Rut. Henceforward there would be no activity in the forest
comparable to that of the first fortnight of October.
And when, a week later, he was up in the glen on a
day with the tops shrouded in mist, all was very
quiet, with only an occasional stag roaring.

One of the latter, however, with a small harem,
lowed incessantly—he was not able to roar—while
walking and running a young stag off his ground.
Then he returned to walk round his hinds and even
to lick the face and ears of one for several minutes,
she responding by licking the musky "tears" trickling
down his face from the glands below his eyes. Usually
hinds objected to these stag endearments, shaking
their heads petulantly, though the watcher could
not recall ever seeing a hind bite a stag.

The timid approach to the hinds of young stags
was in marked contrast to the bold and confident
technique of the masters. Halfway down the face
of one hill a young hind was standing, barking at a
stag with six hinds on the opposite hill: her snorting
bark, sharp, incisive, staccato, echoing in a small
way the stag's warning monosyllabic grunting cough.
A small bachelor stag was making his way tentatively
down the hill, a few steps at a time, towards the
hind. Finally he was only thirty yards above her:

but nearer than that he could not summon up the courage to venture, nor even to roar at the other stag.

Despite its apparent volume of sound a stag's roar had no great carrying power. Even under the most favourable conditions on a still day a couple of miles might represent the maximum carry, while on windy days the watcher had found it a common experience to observe a stag going through all the motions of roaring on the crest of a hill on the other side of a ravine, and only 300 or 400 yards distant, and yet be unable to hear a sound. The hind's bark had even less carrying power, but could penetrate wind to greater distances than a stag's roar.

* * * * *

In these closing days of October the deer were passing through a confused transitional stage, from those few short promiscuous weeks, dominated by the stags, to the establishment of that orderly pattern of more or less discreet herds, composed of mutually indifferent hinds and stags, into which they would be divided for most of the remainder of the year.

On the last day of the month the watcher took advantage of a mild day, with the cloud base at 3,500 feet after a week's bad weather, to make the long trek to those summer pastures of the deer from six forests on that eastern upland, located at a height of between 3,000 and 4,000 feet.

It was a three-mile climb up the stalker's path, from the Glen of Crags, lying a little above 1,000 feet, to the summit of the mountain barrier; but long before he had breasted that ultimate, almost sheer

700 feet immediately below the summit bothie, he had observed a sign of the season.

No great distance above a lonely farm-steading in the glen was a spacious corrie, rank with old bushy heather. This corrie was connected by the Pass of the Lochans to another of colossal proportions, the Red Corrie, which swept down almost from the mountain ridge to the pine forest fringing the glen— a dark green belt flecked with little puffs of gold, where frosts had seared the few birches. The smaller corrie, like the pass, was a favourite winter resort of stags, and it was already occupied by eight big stags.

Henceforward he could always be certain of finding stags in the fifty acres of this Heather Corrie, or on the steep slopes flanking the pass, on any day until some time the following June, when all the deer migrated to the high mosses and corries; for though in the weeks before and during the Rut some stags might wander considerable distances, travelling as much as seventy-five miles right across the Highlands from coast to coast, in the days before railroads, making nothing of swimming across lochs and sea-lochs, they were essentially conservative in their choice of summer pastures and winter retreats, and also of their rutting glens, to which the same stags would return year after year; while a wounded stag would always endeavour to reach his home forest, though this might lie many miles distant from the rutting glen, limping on his way tenaciously as far as his ebbing strength permitted.

Cold the deer did not mind, so long as a heavy fall of snow did not freeze solid over the herbage floor; and even under those conditions they could break through the frozen crust of snow covering bushy heather, or thrust their long heads in at an angle beneath it. Hence the perennial attraction of those corries filled with old belly-deep heather, which also made a snug bed if the snow were not too deep; while, in the pine forests, there was good feeding on the no less luxuriant growth of blaeberry, so acceptable to the deer that it was often difficult to find flowers or berries in the summer following a hard frost. Nevertheless, the deer's staple winter foods were the lichens and mosses and berry-plants, which depended so much for fruition on the shelter afforded by the nurse-heather, and these were denied to them by frozen snow in those places where the heather was absent or young and short. Even so, it was in open winters of heavy rains that the deer suffered their heaviest mortality from the ravages of such internal parasites as lung-worms and liver-flukes.

Complementary to the freshest and most vigorous growth of heather in the Highlands was this astounding carpeting growth on the watcher's moors of berry-plants and lichens; for these mid-Highland moors were dry, despite a few peat-hags and sphagnum bogs, with abundant lycopods, scarlet, black and silver lichens, and reindeer mosses. The berry plants flourished especially along the verges of moor roads and on protruberant knolls and flats, seizing eagerly on those burnt areas temporarily or permanently denuded of heather, though never stifling the new growth of that extraordinary plant.

A perfect symbiosis existed between heather and berry, and between berry and lichen; and when the

low winter sun, only just clearing the rounded bulk
of the south-west hills, lit up the scarlet berries of
bearberry and cowberry in vivid little motes of
colour, whole patches of moor, especially little
hollows in the heather, blazed with the red sealing-
wax sporophores of lichens, which thrust up in little
colonies from the mat of bearberry and ashy-green
reindeer-moss. The dominant vegetation on a
gravelly flat at 2,000 feet, this false reindeer-moss
was yet plentiful on the floor of the strath, more than
1,000 feet lower.

*   *   *   *   *

From the summit dome the watcher looked out
eastwards over those 15,000 acres of upland "mosses",
shelving down from the encircling mountain barrier.
On this grey day this wilderness of the old hunters
was a dark tapestry of black peat-hags and sodden
brown sedge on a background of pale tawny pastures,
with a dark green mossy shading on grey cairns and
outcrops, and here and there in high relief patches
of dark lake-red and rich orange-brown sphagnum moss.
A desolate, lifeless waste it seemed at first sight.
But it was not lifeless. No fewer than six eagles
were hunting ptarmigan, hovering and sweeping
from one pitch to another; while on the lip of one
3,750-foot plateau, already fringed with a few
small patches of snow, the tiny figure of a solitary
hummel was silhouetted; and from the immense
punchbowl corries pock-marking the mountain wall,
which fell sheer from the ridge 2,500 feet to the black
abyssal depths of a long loch, the faint belling and
lowing of stags came to the watcher.

But there was no roaring on the upland, nor any chasing and very little chivying among the few deer present, despite the fact that one herd of thirty hinds was accompanied by six big stags, and that there were a few wanderers here and there. These cannot have been very active, for one small, poor-looking stag had gathered around him as many as thirty hinds and followers, who were grazing among the foothills above a lochan lying in a depression almost at the centre of the mosses; though it was true that such a stag might sometimes rout a big stag by the sole quality of "guts." His large harem contrasted with that of two hinds belonging to a big stag with a magnificent breadth of massively sweeping antlers, whose indifference was such that three staggies were tagged on to his harem.

The Rut was virtually at an end, and the excitement of the day was provided, not by the deer, but by wild geese. All day long skeins of geese had been migrating south over the strath, bound for their wintering grounds on the firths, after rearing their young in Iceland. At noon there was geese music over the hummel's ridge, and the watcher looked up to see four gaggles of grey-lags, snowy-tailed and blue of wing, forging over the upland with a cheery honking. Their passing brought sudden life to the silent mosses, with packs of iron-grey ptarmigan "crackling" in all directions, while the deer, both stags and hinds, looked up from their feeding at one gaggle veering over the lochan, turning their long heads right over their shoulders to follow the geese southwards.

*　　*　　*　　*　　*

Stags were still roaring from those high corries in the middle of November; and when as late as the first week of December the watcher visited the Eagles' Glen again, to be challenged by three or four bursts of short staccato barks from a staggie, he found one big stag still in possession of a harem of fifty-five hinds and followers.

There had been a fall of snow during the night, dusting the hills as low as 1,750 feet. But the weather was still open, and most of the deer were feeding high, delaying their descent to midwinter residence in the glens. Two stags, indeed, could be seen sitting quietly in the snow, head and tail to wind respectively, just below the crest of one hill, and barely distinguishable from the black rocks. Grouse were whirling high over them in all directions, as a black eagle, coasting along the ridges, plunged down over the heads of some hinds grazing near the two stags; but though a calf ran towards the eagle, the hinds ignored him.

Down in the sombre brown, soaked glen beneath, three more hinds and a calf were feeding, dun-olive forms in the near-twilight of this gloomy afternoon. A pale dun stag was sitting a little above them, and a couple of hundred yards above him were two more stags, one yellow, the other a dark red-brown.

It was seldom possible to be certain which way the wind blew through these deep winding canyons, which often turned at right-angles within the bowels of the hills; but, so far as the watcher could judge, the hinds were down-wind of him. Nevertheless, he had walked openly over the slope of the hill to within 300 yards of them before one hind saw him, though all this time the dun stag had appeared to be looking straight at him. Head twisted a little on one side, the hind stared at him short-sightedly for a long time, before leading her companions up the hill with a warning bark, with the dun stag bringing up the rear.

The other two stags made to join the hinds, but this the dun stag would not permit, advancing on them menacingly. Man or no man, he was not going to be deprived of his harem, even at this late date; and in the end the other two stags were obliged to tail off behind, as the hinds climbed up and up, disappearing one by one into the snow-mists now swirling around the tops.

For a while after they had gone the watcher stood looking up, following them in his mind's eye, through the cleft in the hills and along the watercourse.

How lonely the hills would be without their red deer.

II

WINTER

QUITE early in December the wind shifted into the north-east, and the watcher prepared to batten down his hatches against the winter storms.

The change of wind was also significant to the deer. The herds of hinds were restless, seldom stopping for longer than a few minutes to graze in one place; yet, for all their disquiet, curiously indifferent to the watcher's presence among them.

A more cosmic force than man was abroad.

Deer could smell snow several hours before it reached their country, and despite the leaden sky and oppressive humidity, it was in fact two days after the shift of wind before the first storm whitened the low ground.

At the outset a soft flurry of white motes twirled down through the clustered tops of the black-green pines, to dissolve on their varnished red-brown limbs or on the tawny matting of pine-needles strewn along the forest rides; and then the green and brown landscape of autumn suffered a sudden change, in ten minutes of driving blizzard, to winter white, with snow dusting the dark foliage and plastering the tall boles.

This first storm found the watcher halfway up the road to the Eagles' Glen, and drove him home. Files of mountain sheep were walking steadily, but purposively, down the long road from the high glen, and the road's snowy surface was patterned with their neat cloven slots and skids. One black ewe with a single horn he recognised with a smile as homeward bound from the highest corrie in the glen.

So, too, in almost any other part of the Highlands, the passes leading to sheltered glens and corries would have been filled all day with strings of hinds coming down off the high ground, and by nightfall many hundreds might have found harbourage in one glen, wooded for preference.

But not in this country, where safe shelter in the pine forest for hinds lay only a few hundred yards below the hill corries; and as for the stags, what did they care for snow! Immediately before the storm broke a circular clump of seventy-five stags were still scraping for mosses on the summit of one 3,000-foot hill.

* * * * *

A level nine inches of snow fell in this storm, and when it had spent its fury, glen and forest lay hushed within the solemn white grandeur of the mountain ring.

The hushed loveliness of the Christmas season was rung in by the mellow bugle-notes of swans, herded on the water-meadows below the watcher's house.

Morning and evening the cold, immaculate hills lay inviolate against a vault of unfathomable lilac-blue. Mountains of gold ore when the sun shone, they softened to pale smoke-blue in the shadow of a cloud. No outcrop of rock or black vent of spring marred their smooth white mantle, sparkling beneath the frosty blue sky.

When early dusk drew in, with snow beginning to
fall again, a peculiar contentment communicated
itself to the watcher, snug with blazing fire of pine
logs in the company of wife and children, his collies
outstretched before the fire. They were alone in a
world of their own, yet very close to the deer, their
nearest neighbours.

When the sun was well up in the morning, companies of stags, one hundred strong, could be made
out with the glass climbing up from the pine forest,
in which they had passed the night, to a height of
2,000 feet or even 3,000 feet on the white hills. All
day their black clumps, conspicuous even to the naked
eye at a distance of five miles or more, laced the snow,
as they basked in the sun or scraped away at lichens
and fringe-moss on exposed stony flats, swept almost
bare of snow by strong winds.

Though there was still ample fodder of blaeberry
and heather down in the glen, a little browned by
frost perhaps, they yet preferred to climb to the tops
for those seemingly dry and dessicated lichens. By
all scientific reckoning unnutritious, this scant fare
provided ample provender for these big beasts.

Hinds, however, did not undertake these winter
climbs. Perhaps the call of the high places was as
much psychological as for the purpose of feeding, for
in the hard days that followed, the watcher observed
that in the late afternoon when the sun, setting behind
the western hills, left the strath in cold shadow, as
many as six companies of stags, totalling some 300
beasts in all, would climb up from the corries to
enjoy the last half-hour of sunshine still lingering on
the heights; and then as the rosy glow faded from

the sgors, leaving them in icy remoteness, they would
come plunging down again through the deep snow
in the hanging corries to the upper fringe of the pine
forest.

If it was to be a moonlit night it would not be
long after this before the first familiar antlered head
appeared over the crest of the hill above the watcher's
house—the most eager, or hungriest, of 200 or 300
stags and hinds from farther up the Glen of Crags,
venturing down onto the lower moors, beyond the pale
of the deer-fence framing the arable lands of the strath.

*   *   *   *   *

On the uplands, 2,500 feet above the watcher's
house, every blade of sedge was furred with a half-inch
ice edge, and the snow's frozen crust broke at every
step he took.

On the mosses, 500 feet lower, the snow cover was
shallower, revealing sprays of crowberry, thrusting
fingers of fir club-moss, and brilliant red tufts of
sedge and bent.

A dead, silent, cold world, this tundra was no
longer inhabited by the teeming herds of summer,
though an odd company of two stags, three staggies
and two hinds, were marching along one 3,000-foot
crest, while a hind and her calf were browsing on
an almost sheer tongue of heather among the screes
just below the crest.

But the main herds were 1,500 feet or 2,000 feet
below; and to the watcher, traversing along the snowy
ridge, the full six miles of the glen were revealed. Its
forests and corries harboured upwards of a thousand
deer, including some 400 adult stags.

Ten miles westward, above the high moorland plateaux, towered those scarred hills empounding the Eagles' Glen. Almost denuded of snow by swirling winds, they presented a sterile lunar aspect; but that glen, too, though all but treeless, harboured nearly a thousand deer, 100 of which were big stags.

It was remarkable that so many deer could disappear in such a comparatively limited area, wooded though much of the glen was. Glass as he might, the watcher could spy only one large herd of hinds, eighty strong, together with a dozen stags, in the great Red Corrie—which also held a stag still with a harem of eight hinds, with a lone roarer above them; while perched like chamois on some black crags, lightly dusted with snow, was another small herd of hinds. Of stag herds only one could be seen, but that a big one of 140 beasts couched in that special preserve of stags, the Heather Corrie beside the stalker's path.

He could not recall ever having seen a hind in that corrie, though the pass through the hills, linking it to the Red Corrie was only a mile and a half in length. Yet the big corrie was common ground for both hinds and stags. During the past decade, however, the majority of the hinds had formed the habit of moving out of the Red Corrie at the end of the rutting season, to foregather with the main herd three miles south at the head of the Glen of Crags, until the breakup of the wintering herds in the spring. Whether this move was the result of persecution during the second world war, or because a large part of the pine forest in the Red Corrie had then been felled, he could not determine. The significant point was that these hinds still came down to this traditional rutting place in the autumn.

There were a number of stag preserves in his country. Some were corries in the lower hills: others green flats on forest edges. There may have been psychological reasons causing the hinds to avoid these places, but, more obviously, they were all situated near danger points—a bridle-track, a glen road, a lonely farm.

The hind's sense of danger was more acute than the stag's. Whether she was conscious of it or not, the mature hind had other deer dependent upon her, not only the calf of the year, but older young upwards of three years, while in her particular group might be still older offspring, themselves perhaps with young followers.

The stag, on the other hand, had not developed any strong sense of responsibility for his fellow members of the stag herd—the hummel was perhaps an exception—and he wandered where he listed; though being like all animals strongly conservative in his ground sense, he had those favourite haunts on low ground in winter and on high ground in summer, which had become traditional resorts of his kind.

Bent on obtaining a closer view of the big herd of stags, the watcher slithered cautiously down the steep icy slope. Deer, he knew, did not like men or dogs getting above them: but, on the other hand, they did not normally look for danger from such a quarter. In any case it was one thing stalking a herd of feckless stags, but quite a different proposition a herd of hinds, with She of the Long Ears ever on the alert.

But though the inhabitants of the frozen high

places were few in winter, he found that there were others beside deer with their eyes upon him, as he negotiated the bare slopes.

First it was an old cock grouse who whirred up with a warning "go-back, go-back, go-back", and then a posse of four arctic-white ptarmigan spat their machine-gun bullets at him, as they jinked away over the colossal amphitheatre of the Red Corrie. A raven added his sombre croak to the general protest; and finally a big dog fox, all bushy tail, went lolloping over the dome of a lesser hill immediately above the Heather Corrie.

When, therefore, he ultimately eased himself over the brow of that lower hill, he was not surprised to find all the stags on their feet and alert, though as yet undecided as to the exact nature or location of the danger. As it was now too late in the afternoon for a long stalk, he stood up on the skyline, in sharp silhouette against the white backdrop of the snowy mountain.

At this sudden move there was consternation among the stags.

First the whole herd—of all sizes and ages from staggies to royals—milled around in a deplorable state of confusion and nervous tension: chasing irritably, rearing up on their hind legs, horning one another, and sparring with antlers, heads held low.

Then little groups or individuals began to break away in divergent directions, only to turn and rejoin the herd, still uncertain which way to run—for though comparatively long-sighted and able to distinguish a man at a distance of 500 or 600 yards, deer, like keen-sighted dogs, found difficulty in evaluating the precise nature of any strange object, if there was no favourable current of air to carry its scent to their unfailing nostrils; and, since the watcher stood motionless, he was still indeterminate.

But finally some herd impulse, or perhaps the action of some more dominant stag—no hummel could be seen—did produce order out of chaos, and the entire herd moved in one direction, heading for the pass northwards to the Red Corrie; and a very fine sight it was to see them cantering into the narrow defile, as with heads held high and 140 pairs of antlers laid along backs in a forest of tines—some great heads bearing twelve or fourteen points—they plunged down the almost sheer and fearfully broken siding at full canter without a stumble.

Leaning upon his crook, the watcher followed the herd almost in awe. For how many years had stags wintered in this corrie, and defiled through that same pass? How many countless generations of deer had trodden the same paths over the hills, until they had become well-marked highways, as plain to the observant eye as Roman roads? Not that the deer's highways always ran straight across the hills and through the glens. On the contrary, deer paths were often circuitous, following always the least precipitous, and often the only possible routes across steep and shifting screes and bare slabs of rocks, selecting their pitch where the angle of incline was least.

Moving normally in single file, each deer following the peach-coloured heart-shaped blazon on either side of its fellow's tail, thousands of hooves had consolidated firm narrow ramps across the screes, and

had trodden prostrate, year by year, the tough woody
stems of old heather. Only the accidents of frequent
spates and landslides interrupted the perpetuity of
their highways. If a man were lost on the hills in
mist he would come to no harm if he followed the deer
paths, though some there were across the screes that
would test his nerve to the utmost.

It might be necessary for the top wire of a deer
fence to be eight feet above the ground. That was a
measure of a marauding stag's capabilities, assisted
by drifting snow. But it was only the hungry stag,
the stag in rut, and the stag hard-pressed by the hunter
who were responsible for the famous "leaps", of twenty-
five or thirty feet, of deer lore. Traversing the hills
on their everyday business, deer sought the easiest
way round any obstacle, crossing the steep burn-side
or rocky gorge at those places which a man could
also negotiate with comparative ease. Both had a
good eye for country. But few crags could defeat
them, if hard-pressed, and a hunted stag would go
down a sheer cliff on its hindquarters.

*   *   *   *   *

As the watcher went down into the deserted
corrie's shelving amphitheatre, waist-high in very
old heather and floored with spongy clumps of
sphagnum moss, he perceived that the stags had
checked their headlong rush, obeying another herd
impulse, or perhaps following the erratic swerve of a
leading stag.

Leaving the pass, they were circling back, up and
across the face of that hill from which he had descended.
No longer panic-stricken, each stag in turn stopped

on reaching the pony path, either to browse on the
luxuriant growth of bell-heather fringing its gravelly
edge, or possibly to scent at the path, untrodden by
the watcher; and by the time he had finally quitted
the corrie, the whole herd had climbed the hill into
the last of the sunlight, and were couched down, at
peace once more, on a big patch of heather clear of
snow.

It was a strange experience to come down from the
mountains in the heat and full light of day—for the
sun had been hot up there on this still frosty day—
and yet to trek homewards the five miles across the
moors into a smoky fiery sunset, which threw a
lingering rosy glow on the white crests behind.

But the moon was in its second quarter, and for
the deer the day was not ended. Every advantage
must be taken of light on these short winter days to
feed while they might. From the pine forests and
hanging birch woods at the southern head of the glen
another big herd, both hinds and stags, were straggling down onto the moors, to feed along the watercourses of the shallow moor glens, while the moon
was up.

Well in the van were the big stags, more adventurous, less cautious of possible danger than the hinds—
typical male animals. They would feed furthest
afield during the night, up to eight or nine miles
distant indeed from their home glen.

But there were wanderers among the hinds too.

On more than one midwinter day the watcher had
come upon a lone hind, with calf and yearling, almost as far from home as any of the stags; and during
those impressive migrations preceeding snow-storms, a

hind and her yearling might appear in a glen which had not harboured deer for some years, and five miles distant from the wintering glen. He found it difficult to believe that a hind could lose herself, but no other solution was apparent, and was in some degree confirmed by the hesitant, veering course such a hind would follow.

* * * * *

On Christmas Day the watcher noticed that the herds were again restless, and the hinds irritable, not allowing him to approach them closely.

The portents of a fresh, with its attendant discomforts of fluctuating temperatures, strong wind, driving rain and burns in spate, were as perceptible to the deer's acute senses as the oppressive conditions presaging snow. But a thaw would also bring better feeding on fresh mosses and berry-plants, which had been protected from frost by their snow covering. So, if irritable, the deer were also active.

The westerly breeze of the morning freshened to gale force, carrying torrential rain from the Atlantic. By evening every scrap of snow had been washed off all the ground below 1,500 feet, and black patches sullied the snows at twice that height.

As he went up the hill over the moors the next morning he saw that the forbidding black and white mountains were no longer a part of the strath world, with its pleasant warmth of colouring—deep green moss in the pinewoods, deep lake-red heather, paler pools of brown and rose-coloured "deer's hair" bents in the bogs; while the deer, who had stood out so conspicuously against the snowy hills, were once more lost

among the heather, except when a gleam of sun
pricked out, like so many grey stones, the pale masks
of a herd of stags, couched on a steep hill face.

The first of them that forenoon was a herd of twenty
stags couched on a 1,700-foot ridge north of the hill
road, their antlers silhouetted against the sky, their
tawny bodies not immediately perceptible on the
brown hill. The finest antlers among them resembled
a curved W in outline, the moderate heads were U-
shaped, the poorest almost bulging Vs, so narrow was
their span; while in one case an abnormal prolong-
ation of the in-curving tips of the beams produced the
illusion of a closed elipse. By those wide spans and
those arched beams, "wind-blown" in bold, sweeping
curves, might stags of the high places be known.

Stags, but much less often hinds, commonly couched
on the skyline, and consistently walked along hill
crests, commanding in either case a wide field of
view over open country. This strategical advantage
they exploited to the full, tactically, by almost
always facing to all points of the compass, when
resting—too invariably, the watcher had come to
the conclusion for these tactics to be a matter of
chance. Had they adopted this strategy during the
few hundred years that man had stalked them over
the Scottish hills? It was only three or four hundred
years since wolves had hunted them. Surely their
defence then lay in harbourage in the forests that
clothed the greater part of the Highlands below 2,000
feet.

He considered this phenomenon again, and for
the hundredth time. Hinds, no less than stags, were
always to be observed facing in all directions when

resting. Such an arrangement *must* be a matter of chance, for obviously a hind did not cast a critical eye upon the various positions of her fellows before she plumped down. Yet he could not recall a single instance in which all the members of a herd had sat facing one way, no matter how few their numbers; but the law of averages demanded some exceptions to this rule, if such an arrangement was in fact one of pure chance. Deer couched down in order to chew the cud, not to rest, though they might doze while cudding. Rest periods were governed presumably by digestive requirements. Although deer were continually on the move while feeding, often crowding into bunches, there were always one or two in the herd lying down cudding, one following another at short intervals; and the watcher doubted if he had ever seen a herd of more than twenty deer all feeding together for more than a few minutes at a time—except, perhaps, during severe winter weather. While a higher proportion of the deer were to be seen feeding in the evening and early morning, there was no hour of the day, and probably night, when some were not feeding. Thus, it was seldom possible to watch a herd of stags or hinds for longer than a few minutes without observing one deer get up to feed or another sit down to cud; but it was rare to watch a hind couch for more than half an hour at a time. So, too, while during one two-hour period most of the members of one group of stags might be resting high up on a hill face, in the lee of its crest, another group of the same herd would be feeding in the corrie below throughout that period.

The problem remained.

Two of the twenty stags were resting in a hollow
several hundred yards distant from their fellows,
and were also facing in opposite directions across the
wind. One was a young staggie with brow points
only, the other an eight-pointer. The watcher was
within fifty yards of the two, before the staggie became
aware of his presence and springing to his feet,
trotted this way and that indecisively, before galloping
off; but the older beast, though getting to his feet
on the departure of his squire, did not observe the
cause of his alarm, and stalked only slowly away,
feeding up-wind as he went.

A bend in the road brought the watcher up-wind
of two more stags some 250 yards distant, and again
it was the smaller stag who caught his direct scent
immediately, and was away in a hurry. Though deer
were reputed to be able to wind a man at a distance
of one mile, they could only do so when a strong wind
was blowing directly to them over open ground.
Normally one could approach down-wind to within
half a mile of any herd of deer.

The association of a big stag with a youngster
presented another problem of deer behaviour. It
was quite a feature of stag life, but it was questionable
whether it was a deliberate choice by the master of a
squire to keep watch for him. Young stags followed
their elders within the herd, and would do so naturally
when individuals strayed as they grazed, and this
probably accounted for reports of squires accompanying big stags on their rutting travels; while on those
occasions when a stag had been wounded and, after
running with the herd for a few hundred yards, had
been forced to turn aside and lie down in some hollow,

it was almost invariably a young stag, or stags, who
would subsequently leave the herd and return to
stand near him, keeping him company for several
hours.

*   *   *   *   *

Above the main herd the watcher could now see
the black spires of a pine forest, the Black Wood,
which climbed up the reverse side of the ridge from
the Glen of Crags. This wood was a regular winter
resort of a herd of mainly young stags; since it was
also a fact that stags tended to associate in approxi-
mate age groups, with the younger beasts likely to
be found on the lower and more sheltered ground,
and the hardy veterans in the hill corries and on the
high barrens.

Nature, in her sporadic and indiscriminate seeding
of this wood, abhoring the close and regular planting
of man the forester, had provided the majority of
her children with ample growing room in which to
thrust out and up both lateral and vertical branches.
Dividing perhaps only three feet or six feet above
the ground, the splendid gnarled trunks of these
old pines, forking and reforking, thrusting up candel-
abras of huge limbs, resembled massive holly trees.
Felled in parts, the heart of the forest had now become
a morass of choked watercourses and bushy heather,
through which a man waded with difficulty, and a
dense tangle of spindly blaeberry, brushwood, twisted
limbs and fallen trunks, with here and there pockets
and copses of younger pines and shrubby junipers
rising ten feet in height.

What more perfect harbourage could any roe deer

desire? None. So the wintering herd of red stags had to share the Black Wood's 700 acres with as many, or more, roe deer as could be found in any wood of comparable extent in all Scotland; and on this calm and sunny, mildly frosty morning, with the floods out on their favourite feeding preserves on the water-meadows, the watcher could make out with his glass between twenty and twenty-five roe feeding out on the moor in family groups—for in their natural habitat and where not persecuted, roe were not nocturnal in their habits, and were to be seen abroad, both in and outside the woods, at all hours of the day. They might have been peccaries, so much higher were their rumps than their shoulders.

The previous winter there had been an afternoon when twelve roe had bounded across the hill road before him, one after another; and then all that could be seen of them were twelve white lanthorns bobbing and weaving over the dull moor, and over the fence, and away up to the Black Wood crags a mile distant—disembodied will o' the wisps; but as he crossed their leaping place a wave of musky scent had reached him.

So, as he made his way into the wood, it was more or less inevitable that he should be welcomed by the familiar Y of interrogation of a sleek mousy-olive doe watching him from beside a juniper bush, the length of her neck accentuated by her curious gorget of yellow-white half-collar above a square patch of the same colour.

200 yards further in were two fawns, who ran *away* from her, and she did not bark. Roe fawns were nearly always to be found in pairs, with or without

their parents. Twice the watcher had seen triplets —once, the three yellow fawns only towards the end of November, and again, another year, at mid-September when a doe and three fawns had been feeding out on the water-meadows. On sighting the watcher's collie the doe barked and all three fawns ran to her, before bounding stiff-legged to the sanctuary of a larch grove on a bluff at the edge of the meadows. Later the doe ventured out to feed again, leaving the fawns sitting among the trees.

The watcher's opinion was that in either case he had seen triplets, and that there was small likelihood of one fawn being a fosterling.

*   *   *   *   *

The buck was a further 400 yards distant, browsing among the withered bracken under a pine, on the top of which a cock capercaillie was perched. The watcher was close enough to see the vivid small points of red about the great bird's eyes, and his bright yellow beak, which together with his white shoulder-flash and the metallic dark-green patch on his breast, high-lighted his sombre black plumage.

The buck had a broken foreleg, but this injury did not prevent him from bounding away fleetly when the watcher was fifty yards up-wind among the trees; and it was only on the buck's departure that he realised that the herd of young stags were feeding—it was now noon—on a green oasis among the heather on the lower fringe of the forest.

Wrinkled with the tumbled walls and buried foundations of the houses and sheep-folds of the old township folk, whose green fingers still touched the grassy sward and whose great ash-tree still stood guard against misfortune, this pleasance was a favourite resort of wintering stags. Eastwards they had a spacious view over the moors to the Red Corrie, wherein most of the big stags wintered.

At the watcher's stealthy approach through the forest, there was a little uneasiness among the stags, resulting in some slight aggressiveness—one running cantankerously at another: two getting down to a shoving match with their antlers, the bigger beast pushing the other back several yards with a sudden burst of furious energy, whereupon the latter immediately broke away.

Thirty-four stags there were, all as yet in good condition, in this herd, and only two bore antlers with more than eight points—not that the number of tines was any guide to a stag's age, for a four-year-old might carry eight points; but as a stag aged, so his antlers thickened and their span widened.

Red deer? Not at this season! These stags registered every colour shade from sandy-yellow to dun or dark brown—not quite matching the bleached yellow of the bog herbage, nor the rusty brown of the heather—while there was much indeterminate black markings on their flanks; and if some of the staggies were reddish about the shoulders, the short manes, or rather ruffs, of older beasts were olive-dun, and their faces so pale as to appear greyish-white or yellow.

From time to time one would raise his head for a brief gaze into the driving snow—which had now begun to fall again—slanting across the watcher's front.

Was there a more majestic animal than a heavy-antlered stag, standing at gaze with proud, lifted head, against his mountain background, the breath from his flared nostrils forming jets of vapour on the cool air, as moist sensitive nose tested the wind?

He was the very spirit, the *genus loci*, of hill and forested glen. No human vision could have devised for them a nobler inhabitant.

With the watcher sitting quietly within the fringe of trees, some 250 yards distant, the stags' disquiet was quickly allayed and they resumed their everyday activities, feeding forward steadily through bog and heather. Dainty feeders, stags, picking here and there, but on the move all the time, hind-leg brought forward, fore-leg advanced, ears pricked. From time to time a head would be lifted to gnaw at those places where warble-fly grubs were eating their way upwards all along the spine to the root of the tail, preparatory to emerging later in the spring to pupate in the soil; while ever and again one would shake his head and long ears, and ripple his coat like a dog, revealing rolls of fat, to rid himself of the melting snow, before sinking down on his knees for a few minutes' cudding.

Though one trim little six-pointer, with antlers so white that he might only just have shed his velvet, favoured the heather, browsing the tops of some belly-high "bushes", most of his fellows pushed their heads well down into the heather, and one big dark-brown "switch", with very long brow tines and sharp white points to his beams, fed for some minutes on the pale green moss around a spring, plucking it with upward cut of bottom fore-teeth.

Once settling down to feed in earnest, they did so peaceably enough, though infrequently a staggie would dart forward out of the way of a big fellow. The young six-pointer and the switch were on friendly terms, and at one point the former walked slowly across to the switch and hesitantly invited him to tangle horns. The switch duly accepted, and for two or three minutes the two of them locked antlers very gently, turning bowed heads from side to side.

It was remarkable that a stag was not more often pierced in the eye by his opponent's antler points, particularly when the latter were as spiky as the six-pointer's and as long as the switch's brow-tines; though ears, it was true, were often split in rutting clashes.

Their engagement was one of mutual pleasure, with no show of force or ill-tempered lunging, though a little instinctive manoeuvering on the part of the switch—for stags always endeavoured to push at an angle when fighting, and get through to that un-protected flank. Despite the delicate finesse displayed on this occasion the bony rattle of fencing antlers was clearly audible to the watcher, before the two friends as gently disengaged and resumed feeding.

How remarkable it was, he thought, not for the first time, that all these male animals should herd together peaceably for the greater part of every year. But the facts were, of course, that stags were neuter, rather than male, throughout their lives except during the annual period of the Rut; and that the very existence of the stag herd would become impossible if its members fought so much among themselves as to interfere with the daily round of feeding. As it

was, the stag was an unexpectedly sociable animal.
The rutting season excepted, a lone stag was a rarity,
and nearly always a cripple or a very old beast.

Their toleration of one another was considerable,
and the watcher observed with amusement one small
stag chewing at the tips of a companion's drab-brown
antlers for several seconds—and remarkable antlers
they were, this seven-pointer's, curiously angled, as
if they had been jointed in a series of straight seg-
ments, with the terminal points of the beams sloping
inwards. If not a mark of affection, this act was yet
as pleasurable perhaps to both stags as had been that
delicate fencing with antler tips of the six-pointer
and the switch, so sensitive were these extraordinary
adornments—at other times apparently insensitive
to the most fearful blows.

*   *   *   *   *

By two o'clock all but two of the thirty-four had
lain down in the heather to cud, some very snugly
indeed, with only their grey heads or white faces
visible; and one old eight-pointer, with dark-brown
antlers, couched head-on to the watcher, presented
a most grotesque appearance, his snow-white face
being scored with irregular grizzled markings.

Though all sat facing, inevitably, to various airts
they were not very much on the alert, and though
some heads were lifted when a sheep wheeled around
and trotted across the mossy green on their flank,
none observed the watcher's small movements within
the trees. Moreover, crouching from tree to tree,
a few yards at a time, he made his way to within a
hundred yards of them, and could have got right up

to the outliers, had he chosen to wriggle over the
snow through the heather. He was content, however,
to squat beside the last pine, for his way had always
been to let the deer come to him, when possible. It
was a policy that had paid handsome dividends in
getting to know deer.

At this point he noticed that the nearest outlier,
a shaggy yellow staggie with brow-tines only, was
looking intently in his direction. He took no particular care to remain motionless, and after a few
minutes the staggie got to his feet and moved away a
few paces. At this, the remainder of the herd also
got up, with some reluctance, and after a long stare,
trotted and cantered off a few score yards with their
customary swinging indecision, veering now to one
side, then to the other.

On a one-antlered stag swerving violently out of
the path of one of his fellows the watcher saw that
he was a cripple. An old stag, his single left antler
long, thick, rounded and blunt at the point, he was
suffering from a dislocated left hip. When he walked
the bone could be seen slipping right back, and though
he was able to canter by bouncing both hind-legs
together, he soon gave up the attempt to keep pace
with his companions and turned off by himself into
the forest.

The herd had not been much alarmed, and the
bigger stags, bringing up the rear, stopped to stand
at gaze on a knoll, when the watcher moved out of
the trees into full view, and they were still at gaze
when he walked slowly back into the forest and up
the hill.

*   *   *   *   *

A week later, after more snow had fallen, he found
that the herd had sought a new grazing on a felled
flat higher up in the forest. At three o'clock they
were feeding on blaeberry, heather and moss among
the tangle of fallen logs, brushwood and young trees,
undisturbed by a series of gruff rolling barks from a
roebuck, whom the watcher had startled from a little
pond within the trees at the edge of the flat; and
heedless of the clucking warning notes of a dozen
blackcock, which had flown off the berry-covered
slopes to perch high up on the bare snags of some
tall dead pine gibbets. Very handsome they were
in their blue-black plumage, set off by the dark-red
"scimitars" above their eyes and the white curls to
their lyre-shaped tails.

The watcher himself was within forty yards of the
nearest stags before he was aware of their presence:
close enough indeed to see the jagged cicatrices raised
along their spines by teeth gnawing at the warbles.

One stag was enjoying the sensation of tangling his
antlers with a broken branch hanging from one pine
still standing, lifting up his head to scratch his face
and nose on it. After a minute or two, however, he
was driven away by a second stag who, character-
istically, wished also to endulge in this pleasant
entertainment.

This was a novel variant of that essential property
in most deer forests, the rubbing tree. This was
always a conifer, usually a pine, and often an outlier
on the moorland fringe of the forest—though indeed
all the pines spaced at intervals beside a deer path
leading from forest to hill might be used as "rubbers"
by both stags and hinds in greater or lesser degree.

A favourite tree might be an ancient "rubber" with
all the bark worn off a bole smooth and polished; it
might be barked on one side and polished on the other,
or it might be a new tree fully barked, with long stiff
hairs adhering. Certainly the rough and corrugated,
scaly bark of an old Caledonian pine should prove a
most efficient scratcher, and perhaps its strong spicy
aroma was repellent to flies . . . But, no, in pinewood
bogs was to be found the optimum density of every
kind of insect from midge to dragonfly.

As the afternoon drew on most of the stags gradually
lay down to cud, long tongues curling into nostrils;
and one six-pointer usurped an eight-pointer's couch
without any obvious act of aggression, not even a sly
dig in the rump with his antlers. No, on his advancing
toward the other, the latter sprang up, abandoning
his seat. No doubt there was something menacing
in the six-pointer's attitude, imperceptible to the
watcher, but of significance to his fellow. The six-
pointer did not scrape, but snuffed at the couch for
some time before settling down.

Then, all was peace. Sphinx-like heads, with
pleated manes almost dark-green in colour, were
elevated above the brushwood, observing all ap-
proaches, though from time to time long-lashed eyes
closed, the sun being hot, or an antler would be
turned back to scratch lazily along the spine.

Behind the sphinxes a serrated frieze of spiring
pines, black against the white mountains, in whose
snow-clear gullies of blaeberry a dozen big stags had
been feeding at noon.

Absolute silence. Not even a grunt from the stags.
Not a bird sound, save once when a monstrous

capercaillie swished overhead, and zoomed high over the canopy of young pines in a mile-long glide.

But ever in the watcher's ears, alert for the slightest dissonance, were the still small voices of summer song-birds and of the cuckoo.

A trick of the hills.

Among the stags was a hummel, wolf-like of head and mane. With three or four other stags he had grazed his way up to some crags immediately above the watcher on the south side of the flat, and had been the last to relax and couch down. When, after forty-five minutes, the watcher was contemplating approaching more closely to the main herd, now scattered over a wide front, he glanced up to perceive the wily old hummel couched on the extreme edge of the cliffs, looking fixedly down at him.

The stag had not the long dished face of the hind. Thus side face (grey-white, but black of eyes, velvety nose and inside edges of ears) the hummel's profile, without antlers, was very blunt and square. With his whitish lower jaw and throat, he put the watcher in mind of some quizzical old billy-goat—and how a wild-goat would have delighted in such a situation.

True, the hummel had not as yet defined the watcher as anything actively dangerous, but there he just sat, heedless of the mewing of a pair of buzzards circling over him, like gigantic eyed-hawk moths, and with a full view of the watcher lying on the reverse slope of a small hillock.

The latter, though appreciating the humour of his plight, could do nothing to remedy it; so, by way of a diversion, he tested the stag's reactions to sound, whistling first softly and then loudly. Those cudding seventy yards distant turned their heads briefly on both occasions, no more; but had he tapped his boot against a rock their response might have been very different. Then, tying his handkerchief, a white one, to the handle of his crook, he stuck the latter in the ground . . . but no one was interested, though the hummel stopped cudding.

In the end the watcher slithered backwards into dead ground from the main herd, but was duly spotted by the hummel, whose steady watch had been justified; and on the latter getting to his feet on a commanding position on the crags, the whole herd gradually rose and filed away in good order, disappearing over the northern lip of the flat, bound no doubt for a quiet evening at that green pleasance on the forest's fringe.

*   *   *   *   *

It was six weeks after this, when on his way through the deserted Pass of the Lochans, that the watcher picked up three stags feeding towards its southern end. A dirty dun in colour, they blended perfectly with bog grass and swamp heather on this dull afternoon.

Walking up to a convenient knoll a little more than 100 yards short of them, he lay down to glass them. Two were quickly determined as ten-pointers, but the third kept his head down for some minutes, as he fed along a watercourse; and then, when one of the ten-pointers lowered his antlers threateningly, this third stag plunged away with a halting little shuffle. And yes, there was not a shadow of doubt about it . . . it was the one-antlered cripple with the dislocated hip! What a tenacious hold on life stags had!

A light southerly breeze was blowing down the pass from the stags to the watcher, and by that fortunate act of aggression the cripple's feeding course had been set toward the watcher. Something might come of it. He had always been lucky with deer. So he lay where he was on the steep heather face of the knoll.

Sure enough, though pursuing a somewhat circuitous course, the three stags gradually fed his way, with the cripple well to the fore. Though ragged, all three were in surprisingly good condition, almost rotund indeed; while though he paced somewhat wearily from one feeding place to another, heaving himself out of the numerous cross-burns with a considerable effort, the cripple fed very heartily. Digging his head well down into the bottom of the heather, he often passed his nose over a clump, weaving his head hither and thither, as if smelling out its possibilities, and would go to much trouble to pluck such an insignificant morsel as a single stem of dessicated asphodel; while from time to time he would suck up a mouthful of water from a burn, dribbling messily.

After half an hour the cripple deliberately walked down on to the little flat which lay between the watcher's knoll and the steep face of the opposite siding only twenty-five yards distant, and was followed by the other two. It was only at such close range that the powerful symmetry of a full-grown stag could really be appreciated, with strength in every line and limb, especially in those long massive necks with their coarse thick manes—yellow in the case of the cripple, grey in one ten-pointer, black-brown in the other: a very handsome stag with a dark brown stripe of hair along his spine and a broad bordering of the same colour around the pale copper blazon on either side of his black tail. The youngest of the three, his white-tipped tines were dripping with black peat-moss. In the opinion of stalkers a stag with those dark markings was likely to grow into one of the strongest beasts on the hill.

Poor old cripple! Only the previous day another one-antlered stag, similarly disabled, had been shot hard-by, and the watcher had felt a pang; but here he was, after all. He was no beauty, but he was now so close as to reveal a redeeming feature: a lovely eye, whose dark pupil was encircled—or, rather, "elipsed"—by lucent amber iris, in contrast to the round all-dark eyes of his companions; and for the first time the watcher noticed that he carried a blunt brow-point, only three or four inches in length, while in the place of the missing right antler was a deformed cleft and depressed knob. Sorely afflicted with warbles, he gnawed frequently at the root of his tail, his game leg resting behind and across the hock of the other.

For half an hour the three stags fed abreast of the watcher on this little flat, and never more than twenty-five yards away from him. It really was extraordinary that, with their pronounced lateral vision, they should not observe him lying on his side, knees drawn up, a little above them, as he raised and lowered his binoculars at intervals; nor was there even a momentary cessation of working jaws when infrequently one lifted his head and stared straight at him. And as for

the grouse, resplendent as Highland pipers, with
their scarlet cockades, dark mottled brown fronts,
and white leggings, and indignant at the watcher's
intrusion, not once, not once was a head raised at
their minute to minute cackling and becking, which
echoed from the steep scree immediately above the
stags. Why should there be? Grouse cackled almost
every day of a stag's life.

They had now been feeding for not less than one
hour, probably for very much longer than that; and
finally the younger ten-pointer walked deliberately
off the flat and twenty yards up the heather siding.
There he turned up-wind, and stood relaxed, like
an old horse, cudding for five minutes with that
curious rolling cud of deer, right to left and back
again. Then he turned slowly about, knelt down
one leg at a time, settled his back legs under and
couched facing the watcher, on the same level forty
yards distant, and continued cudding, with eyes half
closed, while his companions went on feeding immediately below him.

Sooner or later these two would follow his example,
and the watcher, now cramped and shivering, could
not lie out much longer. Raising himself slightly on
one elbow he endeavoured to attract the youngest
stag's attention, without disturbing the other two.
In this he was successful, and the former stopped
cudding immediately; but he had to raise and lower
his glasses quite abruptly several times during the
next five minutes before he could induce the cudder,
full-fed and sleepy, to get to his feet.

The other ten-pointer, though not the cripple,
observed this move, and stood looking up at his

fellow fixedly, while the latter, for his part, shook his head, as if he just could not believe his eyes, and looked helplessly down at the other. Then he glanced across at the watcher and, after shaking his head again and looking down at his companion, walked slowly up the hill.

The watcher now sat up and caught the eye of the cripple, who also gazed up at him wonderingly, without stirring; and he had to make a number of slight moves before all three ultimately trotted off the way they had come, the cripple plunging uphill with remarkable celerity, despite that flapping hind-leg; and the last he saw of them was the cripple watching from a high ridge above the Heather Corrie.

But a couple of weeks later he met them again, feeding this time with a herd of seventy stags within that sanctuary corrie. There were two other cripples with broken forelegs in this herd, for stags did not persecute their wounded fellows, once the Rut was over.

*   *   *   *   *

It was the New Year the watcher feared: for Winter seldom deserted his icy lair in the mountains before Christmas. And it was on the third day of the New Year that a blizzard drove out of the east for eighteen hours.

Within a week the snow wreaths on those roads exposed to the north and east were six or eight feet deep, and men walked through narrow cuttings or ski'd along the dyke tops above.

Every morning the watcher and his small sons

shovelled away the snow that had fallen during the night, clearing paths to wood-shed and cattle-byre, in which the collies slept snug in their thick hay-bed; though a drift, climbing ten feet to the byre roof, served a useful purpose, enabling the watcher to ski freely in and out of his garden over the buried fence.

But the snow was only a prelude to winter's white devilry.

The storms were followed by a frost the like of which no man living in the strath could remember—a frost so intense that the pinewoods lost their contrasting blackness beneath a dusting of powdered hoar-frost, leaving the purple-brown of the birch-woods the only colour on the smooth white landscape, before they too were veiled.

The thermometer fell to zero, and then to fifteen below.

The leaden, gummy white frost of the morning hours, before the sun dispelled the rime, caught at a man's breath and bound his moustache with icicles; and the watcher, though sweating profusely while sawing up pine logs, found the steel bow of his bush-saw sticking to gauntleted hand.

At midnight the iron-hard road through the glen sparkled with the diamond-pointed refractions of a myriad glittering stars, and cold moonlight flooded the white mountains with a radiance as bright as day, revealing every precipice in the black-fanged corries.

To the mellow hooting of wood-owls was added the mysterious tremulous yodelling of slim eared-owls. These were friendly sounds of the icy night; but it was at this hard midwinter season too, that the tortured screeching of the vixen, seeking her mate, made the hair creep on a man's nape. There was only one sound more horrible in the glens—the screaming of a hedgehog trapped in cruel steel-toothed gin.

Though the spring from which the watcher drew his water still flowed, the river that cascaded riotously down the steep gorge of the glen, to join its sea-going parent, winding through the water-meadows, now an icy fen, bore an almost solid roof of ice a foot thick, while its falls were imprisoned with pallisades of immense icicles the thickness of a man's thigh.

The fresh snow on the ice-floes near the old stone bridge was a maze of otter's neat tracks, and at a bend in the river, where the current was swift, the watcher came upon a heavily be-whiskered otter tearing at the head of a big salmon on a frozen bank of shingle at the edge of a glacial-green lead of open water. Very cat-like she was, with humped back and pointed tip to long curved tail. Her hunger satisfied, she walked smoothly into the pool and vanished.

At first light every morning a roe deer, who dwelt alone in a black fir spinney up the glen, would cross the river to drink at the spring. Three times one morning the watcher met her stepping casually up the wooded path. Once he was within forty paces of her, as she stood watching a sheep, with her diamond-pointed black-edged ears pricked; and before bounding away, she paused to stare at him with round black eyes, one foreleg raised defiantly.

*   *   *   *   *

From six inches to a foot of snow now covered the
frozen moors, laced with the brown under-sweep of
long heather and glinting with the brilliants of
countless winking heliographs, as the shivering ice-
flakes, fringing every stem of sedge and rush, presented
their fragile mirrors to the sun.

Under the blue sky flawless mountain slopes
glittered with ice-shine; but grey-blue shadows softened the smooth enamelled white hollows of corries.

As the watcher rested on his ski-sticks, gazing over
the endless white pall of moors and rounded foot-hills
to the snowy mountain peaks and ranges, he heard
the musical bell-notes of a dancing flight of snow-
buntings, driven down from their winter haunts in
the mountains.

In the windless woods the snow lay very deep, and
most of the roe-deer had been driven out onto the
moors in their search for food. For some time the
watcher lay on the side of a small knoll, only thirty
yards distant from a buck and a doe and their two
mouse-coloured, grey-brown fawns, who were nibbling
at the heather tops—that life-saving heather—on a
boggy flat; but ultimately, after scraping at the snow
a few times, all four sat down to cud, moist black
noses contrasting with white muzzles.

Later in the day he found the male fawn wandering
about the moor on his own, his ears moving backward and forward as if he were trying to locate
something. Wondering what he was up to, the
watcher eventually found him couched in a boggy,
bushy hollow a few yards away from the buck, who
was also sheltering behind a bush. Perhaps male
fawns preferred the company of their fathers.

These lower moors, a mile or two from home, were intersected by endless labyrinths of peat crumbles, in which hundreds of white mountain hares had sought shelter from the storms. Their beaten trails criss-crossed snow and frozen lochans in all directions, but the peat-lanes were their special playgrounds. Turning corners in the lanes, the watcher was continually flushing them from icicle-hung recesses in the banks. Although all were blue-furred to a greater or lesser extent, with a little brown mottling on necks and ears, he found it impossible to pick them up against their snowy background, until they stretched away almost from his feet, for they appeared dazzling-white at any distance; but after loping off a few yards they would sit up on their hunkers, with characteristic unconcern, and wait for him to approach them once more.

*   *   *   *   *

And what of the red deer herds?

The stags had forced their way through the deer fence, and three had harboured for a night in a pinewood morass close by the watcher's house. Others had broken into stackyards and root-fields up and down the strath, in desperate attempts to stay their hunger; while in one place on the moors, where a great cairn of rocks offered some shelter, a rushy hollow had been flattened by the couching of many stags, lying very close together. Fortunately for the deer there were few winters when falls of rock or drifting snow did not break down the fence in one or more places.

There were deer everywhere on the moors, and the

watcher was constantly having to by-pass stragglers from the herds, and was continually coming upon small groups of hinds and larger herds of fifty or sixty stags. In some cases there would be just a hind and her calf, but more often a hind group would also include a maiden hind and a staggie. Lagging hinds linked the two herds, among them a single young hind with a very small stub-faced calf—so small that he must have been an autumn baby. Poor little chap, he seemed far gone and could hardly raise a trot after his mother, though from time to time she stopped to look at the watcher, only seventy-five yards distant, unalarmed.

Hunger had indeed tamed the hinds, and they would stand gazing apathetically at him, as he circled them at a range of no more than twenty-five yards. They rested frequently, standing or couching down, licking each other's faces and backs sympathetically. Their greyish faces, immensely long and anvil-shaped with mulish ears, contrasted with their dun coats, which gleamed a sandy rufous in the wintry sun.

At noon, one herd of seventy-five big stags were feeding on both sides of the deer fence, only a few hundred yards from a herd of about the same number of hinds and followers. The latter included one staggie or small stag to every six hinds, and also a few big stags. One of these bigger stags approached one hind after another, but got the cold shoulder, the younger hinds spinning around, nose to his nose, doubtfully; for stags were not absolutely indifferent to hinds during the winter and summer. Occasionally one might be seen approaching a hind—or, for that matter another stag—with his head raised a little above the horizontal and his upper lip drawn back from his gums, as he would do when rutting.

Though all hind herds might include adult stags, the watcher made a mental note that he could rarely recall ever seeing a hind in a stag herd. Two of these stags among the hinds, a hummel and a small stag, were cripples, forelegs broken at the knee. Though they moved painfully, the immense length of leg below the knee slapping back, they must yet have been able to travel fairly, for they were five miles from their home glen. If the stalker was a lazy fellow he might overlook these two until they had had time to slough off their broken limbs. Then, they would be able to travel as fast on three legs as their fellows on four, and would rejoin a stag herd. Indeed, stags being clean-feeding animals, and Nature an incomparable surgeon, there was just as good a chance of their wounds healing perfectly; and by the time the next rutting season came round the jagged fracture might have been sealed with hard flesh, with the wound almost invisible externally, and these two might again be masters of harems—though the starvation to be endured this hard winter was against them.

All day the deer fed along the burn-sides of the open moor glens. How many deer the watcher could not estimate accurately, so widely dispersed they were: 500 certainly, perhaps many more.

This coming together in hard times was probably as much psychological as purposive—a mutual sense of comfort in numbers, an apathetic drifting together when their bellies were empty and no choice feeding places remained open in any one herd's special provenance.

One straggling concourse of hinds was gradually making its way down to a spacious flat by a burn-side, where another 150 hinds were already feeding or resting, with scores more on the braes on the far side of the burn, and yet more scores of stags seated on the crest, inevitably, of the hill. As the hinds filed down to the flat, so they would stop in turn to drink at a stream and browse along its edge. Two quarrelled over a drinking place, and with ears laid back, revealing conical polls, and muzzles well raised, they reared perfectly upright, to box futilely with pairs of forelegs slapping up and down with extraordinary swiftness, though without a blow getting home.

Hinds were rather more quarrelsome, or at any rate irritable, than stags, and if two fell out it sometimes happened that their quarrel might continue intermittently throughout the day, in the shape of this harmless slapping of forefeet.

At three o'clock they were still feeding on the flat, scraping among the snow; and they did so in almost complete silence—a phenomenon which impressed itself upon the watcher, in such contrast was it to that pleasant medley of lowing and bleating he was accustomed to hear from the hinds and their calves at their summer pastures. Only twice did a yearling, looking for its mother, utter a series of bleats.

When lying on the side of a knoll, fifty yards from the nearest deer, he was suddenly startled to find in his glass the image of a long-legged staggie walking leisurely round the corner of the knoll. Closer and closer he came, until he was walking out of focus, and right on top of the watcher. The thought flashed through the latter's mind—Could a deer walk actually on to a man? Almost imperceptibly he lowered his glass; and still the staggie came on steadily —fifteen yards, ten yards, twenty feet—and now he was on the watcher's left side and not quite abreast of where he lay in full view on a patch of bare ground, burnt the previous spring, with a light air blowing from behind the staggie.

At this point he stopped dead, and for perhaps three minutes his full dark eyes stared at the un-accountable form of the watcher, who endeavoured, without blinking, to memorise the details of his appearance—the stiff white hairs on his lower jaw, the short greyish ruff, the nine-inch dags projecting from swollen knobs.

What were the staggie's mental reactions during this long period of incredulous indecision? He had almost certainly never before encountered a man at such close-quarters. But suddenly he wheeled about with a snort and disappeared round the knoll in a rush. At his stampede a few of the nearer hinds lifted their heads enquiringly. but lowered them almost immediately, to continue grazing. Staggies would be staggies, and had snorted Wolf or, rather, Man, too often!

As for the watcher, he had achieved an ambition— to shed his physical presence and become a member of deer society. It was enough for one day. Already the evening was bitterly cold. So backing from the knoll into dead ground, without disturbing the deer, he left some still feeding on the flat and others crossing the burn and making their way up the far hill, bound no doubt for the arable lands in the strath.

*   *   *   *   *

Day after day the pitiless frost bound all the deer's country in its steely grip. Only on skis could the watcher reach the mountain uplands now—eight long miles to the summit bothie, though with enough snow to cover all stones and heather and make for smooth going, if he started early and returned late. The stalker's bridle-path, however, now a trough of ice-packed snow, feet deep, which would not melt till the ultimate spring thaw, was so slippery that he had to put skins on his skis before he could get a grip on the snow. Even the ptarmigan were sliding about on the frozen slopes, despite their feathered toes, black tails sticking up jauntily.

Yet the customary herd of big stags, eighty or more, were couched on the long heather of their favourite corrie in the morning sun; and he was astonished to see two hinds and their calves, together with three big stags, crossing the great snowfield, thirty or forty feet deep perhaps, which filled the hanging corrie below the summit crest. Were there no limits to the endurance of these amazing animals?

Two more herds, one of seventeen stags, the other of twenty-three hinds and followers, were browsing on the long heather in the vast amphitheatre of the Red Corrie, over which loomed the smooth white bulk of the ridge in remote and gigantic inaccessibility. When the watcher appeared on the col dividing the two corries, the two herds ran together.

And when he finally reached the summit, at 3,500 feet, there was no bothie. Instead a smooth white glissade of snow had spread an even mantle over the slight depression in which it was sited. A strong wind was blowing, and it was so cold that his collies' coats were instantly frizzed with hoar-frost.

And, for the rest, there was nothing but whiteness, with a faintly bluish ice-shine on all those ranges and peaks rising above the frost-fog in the strath below.

Among the familiar large tracks of mountain hares he was amused to observe, in several places on the steep walls of the Red Corrie and to a height of over 3,600 feet, the neat tiny trails of ermine. No doubt they had come up on the scent of the hares, who had sheltered for the night in snow burries under rocks in the corrie; or perhaps after ptarmigan, who scratched themselves little cups and tunnels in the snow.

He could not recall actually seeing stoats above 2,000 feet. They were the murderous hunters of glens and warrens, perpetrating appalling cruelties upon the unfortunate rabbits; snaking along the runs, nose to ground, investigating one burry after another —snow-white creatures at a distance, during the first three months of the year, though faintly yellowish at close range—chittering with anger explosively at his collies, emitting skunk-like effluvium, from safe retreats in dyke crannies, while poking cobra-shaped heads, with beady black eyes, out and in. In an early spring a snow-white ermine sinuating hither and thither over a bleached tawny bog, pausing time and again to sit up and peep over the tussocks, was as conspicuous an object as Nature had designed, comparable to the dazzling white hare loping over the warm red-brown moor of heather on a sunny March day.

*   *   *   *   *

Sweeping smoothly down across the frozen tundra, the watcher sought in vain for the lochan in the pit of the "mosses." It had become a part of the snow world. Very possibly he had ski'd over it.

A gauzy mist of floating ice-particles was now partially veiling the sun, whose rays were diffused through a dark halo; and in this arctic light the little snow-buntings, running about the snow, appeared almost as white as it and as big as jackdaws, while the white ptarmigan, "reeling" and ticking, were magnified to the bulk of glaucous gulls . . .

On again, across the lonely miles of silent white wastes, and down the winding snow gorge of ghostly ravine to the shelter of a bothie, entombed in the icy womb of the mountains.

Rounding the crags at the end of the ravine he was astounded to see five black figures moving across the snow, down-glen from the bothie—stags! Big fellows, of course; but what were they doing up there in such arctic weather? True, the bothie lay only 2,000 feet above sea-level, but there was no feeding for deer within six or seven miles, nor freely flowing water either for that matter.

They would have to hasten if they were to be down on the low ground before nightfall. Already it was early dusk on the cold white hills and dead black crags, and the frost was barely endurable. On such a night man, and dogs too, needed shelter. Forcing open the door of the bothie, he was thankful to see that the last of its summer occupants had laid in good store of kindling.

The moon was rising, way down behind the great hills on the far side of the glen, her hidden light striking the needled crag of one snowy peak towering above the bothie. And she was still hidden, when her radiance filled the white shells of the high corries, where the deer grazed in summer.

Time to turn in, before her unearthly grandeur lured a man too far abroad on such a night—sleeping-bag on heather couch, feet to fire, dog on either side.

III

SPRING

ALL January and all February the freeze-up held without an hour's thaw, and the watcher lost all sense of reality. Had there ever been a time without frost?

March brought a desiccating wind that burnt up a man's skin, and a fierce sun that melted only the frozen crust of the snow for an hour or two at mid-day. Then he could neither walk nor ski until it began to freeze again in the late afternoon; and on the exposed heights of the moors the north wind was terrible.

Such was the dazzling effect of the strong sun on the white mantle of snow, that it seemed, rather, that a blazing moon shone from a white-hot blue sky; while unreality was heightened by the phenomena of furred motes of hoar-frost sailing through the air, and of a luminous blue light which glowed in the holes made by his crook, and even in such large snow-holes as rabbit-burries; and this unearthly blue light continued to glow in certain places on grey, overcast days.

Unreality again, when entering the dim interior of his house, after a brilliant day on the hills, he perceived a midsummer contrast.

And then, in the second week of March, he awoke one morning to a strange grey light. It was snowing again. But from the south. He knew what that portended. A fresh! Unimaginable thaw!

And now that this for which he had prayed had come to pass he, paradoxically, was seized with a longing to see the deer once more in their winter haunts.

He would visit them in their home in the Glen of Crags.

And this he did, against a driving blizzard of stinging sleet and melting snow. Groups of stags were feeding everywhere in the open birch forest, which climbed a thousand feet from the glen road; and one herd of thirteen younger stags, an eight pointer the biggest among them, was only forty yards above the road. Three staggies saw him, but did not move until he had watched them at leisure and passed by, when they led the herd up into the forest. Farther along were three old stags and a hummel, one lame and a second short of an antler.

The forest was the refuge by day of the young and weak.

At the head of the glen a score of hinds and followers were feeding among the juniper bushes. Shyer than the stags, they filed up the wooded siding without delay. And now he was entering the wildest pass in his country, at that point where the glen narrowed to a canyon, less than 200 yards in width, walled in on either flank by stupendous crags and precipitous screes, which swept down a thousand feet from black battlements, to dark majestic groves of ancient pines, with grassy glades and dense thickets of juniper.

It was with a sense of awe that he entered this Pass of the Crags, whose timeless silence ever cast a spell upon him, treading softly in anticipation of the unknown.

A sudden roll of five or six staccato barks from some impregnable fastness among the broken screes and tumbled boulders, massed with juniper and stunted pines, startled him momentarily—as it always did. Menacing, almost sinister, who would have supposed that this was the warning challenge of that little forest king, the roebuck?

Silence again.

And then as he followed the winding path through the maze of junipers and under the great pines, he saw them in the forest twilight. Shadowy creatures among the pines and prostrate birches, uprooted by falls of rock brought crashing down the screes by sudden spates.

A long muzzle on one side of a tree, the hinder part of another, the tips of two long ears above a log.

In this remote pass one small herd of hinds had found snug quarters. Seldom, he thought, had he found red deer in a stranger place. Some were scraping vigorously at the snow with a forefoot, others couched comfortably against mossy logs. Crouching from tree to tree, he approached to within thirty paces of a three-year-old staggie, who was standing quite still, sleeping on his feet, together with a hind who, mouth half open in blissful vacancy, was rubbing herself in ecstacy against a rough-barked pine, from shoulder along to rump, and from rump back again to shoulder—especially good this way, with back hollowed!

Once again he was conscious of having shed his physical presence.

But camouflaged behind the branches of a leaning willow tree on his left side was another hind. She

was much intrigued by the behaviour of this anony-
mous creature in raincoat and helmet, which peeped
from behind trees and squatted about the snow. The
blizzard, driving down the main glen and over the
crags 1,500 feet above, could not penetrate this
wooded defile. The soft falling snow bore no trace
of scent to her black enquiring nose. For several
minutes, a quarter of an hour perhaps, she puzzled
herself with his identity, staring fixedly in his direction,
intermittently pushing back one long ear in bewilderment; and if she turned her head away for an instant,
she quickly turned it back again.

No doubt he could have played this game with her
all day, granted endurance against cold and cramp;
but from time to time he was compelled to stand
stiffly upright, and ultimately, when endeavouring
to approach closer to the staggie, to cross an open
space between two trees. This move was too much
for the hind, though even then she broke away
reluctantly.

Wanting to find out how many deer there were in
the wood, he now walked forward openly and found
the whole herd assembled on a flat by the river.
Some fifty there were in all, including the one staggie
and, to his surprise and pleasure, after so desperate
a winter, as many as twenty yearlings. Not wishing
to create any further disturbance in their harbourage,
he turned back into the wood and headed for the main
glen, where he found that the storm had passed.

By four o'clock he was abreast of the Red Corrie
hills on the long road home. A few big stags were
still abroad on the sharp inclined ridges of the lower
hills, while others were making their way down to

the shelter of the forest. A white "stone" shining out of a bank of heather, caught his eye. Out on the moor beside the road four roe were feeding. At his coming, first the doe and her two fawns, and then the buck, went weaving and bobbing over the moor and up the brae, like jack-o'-lanterns: for in the dim evening light their dun-coloured forms were swallowed up in the brown heather, and they were spot-marked by the snowy white cushions of hair on their hind-quarters.

Splitting all ways in their bounding flight, more air than ground, causing the sheep to run together and packs of grouse to stream away, the doe, the buck and one fawn assembled on the ridge, the buck's gnarled horns silhouetted against the darkening sky. There they awaited the remaining fawn, who had trouble with the fence, and ran up and down it for ten minutes, searching for a way through the wires.

*   *   *   *   *

He had not been mistaken. A furious fresh wind followed the blizzard, and five days of gales and rains transformed the deer's country into an Arctic tundra: a black, brown and white patchwork of moors backed by white mountains. The frozen roads through the glens were blocked with huge slabs and lumps of pack-ice, forced up from burns and rivers by the spate of melting snows, which stripped the waterside alders of their bark. The sea of tumbled waters on the strath meadows were dotted with ice-flows, which were driven up, one on top of another, on dyke-banks, the only ground not submerged; while those parts of the moors, which had not lain under a deep snow covering, presented a tragically beautiful aspect, burnt as barren by the frost as a beaten earth-floor, with tracts of heather singed crimson and terra-cotta and every shade of brown and chrome.

But it was Spring!

In the birch woods, where a chorus of robins "rippled," swaying and weaving on their perches one before another, the badgers were already abroad, their musky scent perceptible both to the watcher and to his dogs, who were much interested. There were claw-marks on the mound of trampled earth beside the set, and a nearby tree had been scored. They had been opening up a number of holes and rebedding with dead bracken, and under the exposed roots of a sycamore he found their earth-closet, with its heaps of turned earth, little piles of dung and pools of water. When he was looking down into the set, one badger suddenly thundered out of a side hole and down the main burrow in a scutter of speed, flat to the earth. The loamy soil had stained him a curious pale brown.

That roe, who had dwelt alone all the winter, was now running with a buck, whose pronged horns, thickened with velvet, swept up and back like a coronet. Bounding across a glade with giant stride they stretched over the eight-foot wires surmounting the stone-dyke without noticeable effort.

*   *   *   *   *

The week that followed brought new heart to the watcher, as braes and moors quickened. First it was the ever-blessed quavering whistle of a curlew from

over the moor edge, and then the sharp lines of
angular bodies and immense curving bills against
a blue sky. Soon their mournful "whauping" over
the hill above his house was a definite promise of
summer. Then there were peewits wriggling and
buffeting on the pleasant mossy banks and braes,
and tumbling and calling overhead; while from across
the loch sounded the resonant, though dove-like,
roaring of a blackcock. But, most welcome of all,
were the red-billed oystercatchers piping up the
glens and over the fields, running together once
more among the old thorns and boulders.

On the high moors above the Eagles' Glen, where
he had gone to burn heather, the watcher found the
blue hares as numerous as ever, and counted 130
during the morning, with six at a time sitting up on
the front of a fiery line of heather.

An odd thing happened while he was resting from
his labours on the side of a knoll. Not very far away
on the other side of the knoll a solitary stag was
feeding, unaware of his presence; and then, quite
suddenly the stag lay down in the heather stretching
out his head along the ground, antlers laid flat
along his back.

The watcher was much puzzled by this action,
until he realized that the stag was concealing himself
from a shepherd who was approaching. His ancestors
in the woods had gifted him this trick. Nor did he
stir until the shepherd was only twenty or thirty
paces distant, when he jumped up and slid round
the side of the knoll, seeming not to touch it with
his hooves, taking the strands of an old march fence
effortlessly in his tremendous "slow-motion" stride.

But though spring had conquered temporarily in the glens, every plant that should have been green on the hill was bleached yellow or white, sapless. On closer examination, however, the watcher perceived that there was the faintest green cast on those areas of heather that had not been frosted, while the roaring inferno of fire, blackening the strip of old diseased heather, left in its desolate wake a multitude of green spears shooting up unscorched. The blackened waste contrasted strangely with white pockets of snow more than a foot thick, frozen solid despite seven days of soft sunshine. Seldom had he looked upon such a sere and unfruitful world at the spring season.

Nevertheless this burnt strip would be attractive to the deer, especially the stags, later in the spring when the young grass came apace—not so much for the green shoots as for the mineral salts, for which in the less restricted days of yore they would often venture down to the seashore tangle at all seasons of the year.

Yet the deer were enjoying life this day, and the watcher, too, could hardly believe that he was in the same world of a few days previously, when he found himself lying in the sun, basking in its noonday heat in the shelter of the glen, under a blue sky painted with the white plumes of docked mare's-tails, while scanning at his leisure a herd of fifty hinds doing the same, and staggies lazily scratching their backs with their antlers. Only a few of the hinds were on their feet at this hour, though high above them a herd of big stags were feeding at 3,000 feet along the edge of a mile-long cornice of snow, which

projected from the upperlip of an immense punchbowl corrie—a traditional stag sanctuary. The
broad cornice was scored by their maze of tracks.

An eagle was circling above them. And then
there were two. With golden beaks gleaming in the
sun, they lunged playfully at each other on rocking
wings, or rolled over on to their backs, with wings
widespread; then plunged headlong with grappling
talons; before ultimately soaring leisurely up and
away from one another in sweeping arcs.

Smooth and deliberate was their majestic sailing.
Incomparably powerful and buoyant, swift and
effortless, their soaring, with never a beat of those
broad pinions, whose long primary-feathers were
splayed like spread and upturned fingers.

Theirs was the true poetry of motion, communi-
cating itself to the spirit of the watcher, so that he
seemed to soar aloft with them, up and up, until
in the end they sailed away over the tawny moors,
wrinkled with their innumerable deep ravines and
shallow watercourses, and over the shimmering
white lochs, to be lost against a craggy waste of red
scree on a distant hill.

*   *   *   *   *

Another herd of sixty stags were feeding in the
sanctuary corrie—or, rather, thirty-five of them were.
Of the twenty-five resting only grey antlered masks
could be seen above the heather—that rough, warm
mantle, the deer's strong cover. A quarter of a mile
distant, they might just as well have been mounted
heads, for a stag's face and antlers were aligned along
the same vertical axis. But when, after glassing them

for an hour, the watcher was preparing to back away stealthily, the breeze suddenly veered round behind him. Up went a score of heads, ears cupped in his direction; and then the whole herd trotted irresolutely up the back wall of the corrie.

Exactly one hour later, at two o'clock, the watcher, having climbed the hill outside the corrie, came round the back wall and looked down to see the last feeding stag of the herd just sinking down on to his knees. Here was a rare sight! An entire herd of stags at rest. It was grand to see them so, after the long winter, all couched content, cudding in the hot sun, each one a yard or two from his fellow, and facing in various directions, though two-thirds of them faced south with an easterly breeze blowing across their noses. There was, he reflected, no parallel in human society to such communal serenity. Cradled within its nine great hills, distant and mysterious beneath a slight heat haze, this corrie was a place of infinite peace and absolute, timeless silence.

For seven long minutes there was no movement in the corrie; and then the spell was broken when one stag rose to his feet and after sniffing at his couch for a few moments, settled down to face in the opposite direction. Again the herd was at rest, for eight minutes this time, before first one and then two stags got up—only to couch down again within three minutes, as did another who was up three minutes later to feed. But finally, after twenty-five minutes, one got up to gnaw at a warble and then began to feed in earnest; and he was followed during the next nine minutes by two more, and subsequently another two when there was a slight fracas owing to one of those feeding approaching too closely to a companion at rest. Five stags were now feeding; but all couched down again almost immediately except the first to get up, who after a quarter of an hour was grazing out of the circle of the herd.

Half an hour later, at three o'clock, the watcher, passing on north round the hill behind the herd, came down on their flank to find that all had been on their feet for some minutes, for the leaders were now widely scattered, feeding busily into the wind, while the last to get up were just walking slowly down behind them.

Thus this mid-day period of rest on an exceptionally fine spring day had lasted for little more than an hour, with eight minutes the longest interval for all the stags to be couched at one time; and by this time all the members of the hind herd were also on their feet and feeding lazily up the burn-side, crossing and recrossing the rocky bed of the stream, as they made their way into the upper heart of that other corrie, wherein the eagles had their eyrie.

*   *   *   *   *

An April afternoon at the wild entrance to the Red Corrie, from whose precipitous and densely wooded gorge stunted flat-topped pines climbed sparsely over crags and through long heather to a height of nearly 2,000 feet, found stags everywhere. But, as was so often the case, not a hind was to be seen.

The hinds' ability to hide themselves away was remarkable. In all his years with the red deer the

problem of where he might find the various small
herds of hinds on any particular day was one that
the watcher had never resolved to his complete
satisfaction. The fact was that, though less mobile
than stags, hinds were not as sedentary as some
stalkers had suggested. As soon as the spring thaw
made the going practicable and laid bare the bogs,
the winter herds broke up and groups of hinds, some
comprising less than a dozen individuals, dispersed
over the immense wilderness of high moors round
about the 2,000-foot contour, and even penetrated
to the most inaccessible glens in the heart of the
mountains; though the stags continued to haunt
their winter corries and ridges just above the forest,
and would continue to do so until the grass began
to grow on the uplands in May or June.

Thus, on a day in the first week of April one year,
when a severe but short winter had perished of its
own fury as early as the middle of February, the
watcher, looking down from the heights above the
Red Corrie into that fearful chasm on its far side,
2,000 feet below the craggy crest of the ridge, had
been surprised, at that early date, to see several
scores of hinds feeding on the marshy flat at the head
of the long loch that filled this gloomy ravine, four
or five miles from their nearest wintering ground.
Stags he had never seen on the floor of that glen,
though during the Rut wanderers passed through
the glen and up over the mosses to the Glen of Crags
and perhaps as far as the Eagles' Glen.

Moreover, a week before the end of April two
herds, one of forty hinds, the other of seven stags,
had actually been grazing on the uplands, with

another herd of twenty stags resting below the summit
bothie. For several minutes the watcher had leant
against the wall of the bothie looking down on this
herd. Eventually the biggest stag got up to feed,
touching up his neighbour quite gently with his hoof,
and then horning up the rest one by one as he grazed
towards them, until all were on their feet feeding,
unaware of the man and two dogs only seventy
yards above them.

Once again he had striven to fathom the attraction
of those desolate uplands, whose only greenery at
that early date lay in the sprouting hearts of the hard-
carex's sharp sword-blades and on the cushions of
moss-campion, which was not attractive to the deer.
There was richer feeding in the glens than on that
greyish tundra of tindery fringe-moss and bleached
bent and sedge—that dead world, two fifths of which
was harrowed with bare black, wind-scooped peat-
hags, and another fifth scarred with broken grey
outcrops of rocky cairns and kopjes pitted with frozen
lochans. Moreover nine-tenths of the uplands were
normally covered with deep fields of snow at that
season, while the remaining tenth would be water-
logged, with rills of water oozing from the saturated
woolly-moss. And this might be their state until
well on into May or even June.

The only sure draws for hinds in spring were certain
small marshes, black peaty bogs, far out on the moors.
Three miles from the nearest dwelling of man, they
were visited only rarely by a shepherd and his dogs,
but haunted by ducks, while gulls and peewits
nested in their lush cover. Yellow sedge and bog
cotton, whose downy plumes the old stalkers had

been wont to carry with them to test the wind, were the attraction—the earliest green bites in the Highlands.

At first the deer, ten or twelve hinds and followers and sometimes a big stag, would feed timidly at the edge of a marsh; but as the succulent rushes grew, so they ventured further, and it was an amazing sight to see the hinds wading, or rather stepping, thigh-deep through the middle of the marsh, extricating their long legs with considerable difficulty. For the short-legged sheep, weighed down with heavy fleeces, such a marsh was a death-trap.

But it was quite possible to tramp the waste of high moorlands all day at this season and never set eyes on a herd of hinds, or perhaps only be apprised of their presence by the accident of coming upon a shaggy stag calf—for as yet his smooth round poll bore no trace of his first knobs—sitting all by himself in the heather low down on the steep wall of a glen.

As he turns and "stilts" slowly away, stepping delicately, his hind hocks go up very high with piston-like regularity; and when he breaks into a trot, plunging downhill, the drive of those strong hind legs is as tremendously powerful as that of a full-grown stag—more impressively so perhaps, for he has little weight to carry and is all legs.

Stags were more independent than hinds from their earliest days, and knobbers might sometimes be found running with the stag herd; but, in this instance, something would be very wrong if there were no hinds anywhere in the vicinity. All the same the watcher had to climb right out of the glen and on to the high moors, lying above 2,000 feet, before he eventually located the herd of seven hinds, with two more calves, feeding in the bogs nearly a mile distant from the stag calf; and this was the only herd anywhere within the range of his glass.

And so, on that April afternoon in the Red Corrie, it was the more usual tale of not a hind to be seen: but herds of stags everywhere.

First five, and then six, big fellows galloping down from a pass between two heights, sparring a little as they pranced down, to join ten more feeding on the lower slopes among the highest pines; while another herd of thirty, including a hummel, were feeding at the northern entrance to their favourite Pass of the Lochans.

One old stag among these had cast his antlers a week or so earlier, and the dark velvet-skinned knobs of their successors were already apparent. A protective covering to the antlers while they grew, this "velvet," with its abundant blood-vessels, also assisted their growth.

After a winter's semi-starvation, coupled with the continuous drain on their vitality imposed by the parasitism of warble-fly grubs and blood-sucking keds, the stags were at this season in their poorest condition; and it was those most forward in condition, together with the older beasts, who were the first to shed their antlers. It might be the end of May before some of the staggies would cast theirs. Yet seldom was it possible to find a shed antler, much less a pair. The watcher's forest, like most others in the Highlands, was deficient in natural phosphates, and just as the stags were always keen to graze on new grass on burnt ground containing ash, so, too, not a cast antler would be left unchewed from the points down to the very butt, in an attempt to satisfy that craving for the calcium and phosphates of which their antlers were compounded.

He had found that the only way to make certain of collecting a perfect pair of antlers, before they had been chewed, was to watch the stags closely. An antler usually fell off when a stag was feeding, and if one fell, then the stag would shake his head violently and the other antler might fall too. Relieved at being rid of them the stag would toss his head, bound high into the air, and gallop away, leaping from side to side. But more often the second antler did not fall until several hours after its fellow, and in another part of the forest.

It was not only the stags who craved calcium and phosphorus. The watcher had known of more than one hind who had died from the effects of part of an antler sticking in her throat, while both stags and hinds would crunch the legs and skulls of snared hares and rabbits and the bleached skeletons of their own kind. Complete skeletons of deer were even harder to find than antlers, with as many as twelve golden eagles, twenty or twenty-five ravens, and wintering flocks of up to fifty hooded crows, all carrion feeders, working over the watcher's country. A stag's carcass would provide a feast for ten ravens for ten days.

Though there was a tendency for some of the stags to wander away in ones and twos at the time of antler shedding, the daily routine of the majority was not affected by this climacteric. A natural comple-ment to depressed vitality was, however, a lowering of their threshold of fear of man, and it was at this season that they were often easiest to approach. So as the watcher walked up to that herd at the entrance to the pass, there was a long interval of contemplation, before the leisurely move-off, with incomparably majestic high-stepping gait, to climb the almost vertical wall of the pass.

Once again the hummel was in the lead, while staggies were horned up the hill by their elders, their pale brown or dun-yellow forms almost invisible against the dead brown strips of heather reaching down the sidings. Alternately climbing and cantering, they made heavy weather of the 700-foot ascent, tongues lolling out, pinched flanks heaving: for deer preferred to climb a steep slope obliquely, when their small, extraordinarily hard and sharp-edged hooves afforded them a perfect grip on the most precipitous scree.

Another sixteen stags, all young, were couched and feeding at the south end of the pass. Relaxed, full-length, they stretched themselves like cattle when now and again one got to his feet and first arching his back, then flexed forward with hind legs extended and tail lifted, rippling his coat, before walking slowly forward to a deep pool for a long drink—as did five others before they began to feed.

Again it was a hummel who sensed danger first, and was on his feet immediately, while the nearest antlered stag remained couched in oblivious content-ment, even when the watcher stood up in full view only thirty or forty yards distant.

At this move half the herd trotted away round the corner of the pass, led by a big eight-pointer, their fellows following more leisurely; but before the latter had reached the mouth of the pass one of the vanguard re-appeared, to stand on a knoll, as if looking for them.

The watcher knew that he had returned in search of his special friend, from whom he had become separated; for though the sense of herd responsibility was not developed among stags in as full a measure as it was among hinds, the watcher had observed many times that individual stags liked to be together. More often than not such a friendship was between a big stag and a young one.

An old stalker had retailed to him a remarkable story of such a friendship, when three stags had been disturbed from a small wood. Two had jumped their way out over a low wire fence; but the third, a young staggie, had panicked and refused to jump this insignificant obstacle. His two companions had stood waiting on the hill for some time, while he chivied up and down the fence—as that young roe deer had done—and finally the bigger, a ten-pointer, came down to the fence. The staggie ran towards him, and the ten-pointer trotted away invitingly; but, even so, the little fellow could not brace himself to leap that three-foot fence.

Again the big stag came down and, jumping over the fence this time, went up to the little stag and rubbed noses with him several times—"kissing," the old stalker had termed it—before leading the way to and over the fence once more; but all to no immediate purpose, for it was not until his two companions had finally left him and gone away over the brow of the hill, that the little stag ultimately scrambled over the fence and galloped the way that they had gone.

How did deer communicate, one with another, within the herd? Was the herd life of stags no more complex than a perpetual visual follow-the-leader? The hind barked, and that sound was understood by other hinds and followers; but stags were virtually dumb, except during the Rut, when their roar was meaningful to other stags. No doubt a form of telepathic communication existed between one deer and another; but they also expressed themselves by physical contacts—as on that occasion when a knobber and an older staggie had been feeding together, and the knobber had caught sight of a stalker's head peering round a rock some fifty yards distant. For a minute or so the knobber had stood at gaze before trotting up close to his companion's nose and standing at gaze again. At this, the staggie raised his head and looked around, but seeing nothing untoward, resumed feeding. The knobber then moved forward a few paces towards the rock, only to trot back to his companion once more; but this time the staggie did not even lift his head. So the knobber reared up on his hind legs and thumped the staggie on the shoulder with his forefeet. Thus prompted, the staggie looked around for some time, and though still not observing any cause for alarm, ultimately followed the knobber away over a ridge.

Hinds were usually more inquisitive than stags, but on a day later in the month the watcher had an interesting encounter with a herd of thirty-two stags browsing on the long heather just within the upper pines at the head of the Glen of Crags. By this date nearly half the herd had cast their antlers and one or two had pronounced velvet prongs, which, branching almost horizontally, imparted to their bearers a strange and goat-like appearance, a resemblance increased by their whitish-grey masks and manes, pale in the sunlight.

It was a day of intermittent snow-squalls, following a period of blizzards, and a slight veering breeze was blowing not quite directly from the watcher to the herd. Their noses uncertain, their eyes unable to determine with precision the identity of the object squatting in the heather on the hill above, the entire herd advanced, spread out in a wide arc, as if to do battle; and for a fleeting second the watcher was conscious of disquiet at their menacing array.

If the breeze veered more directly, so they shied away, rearing up ill-temperedly, with ears half-lop and heads a little on one side, to box with swift-swinging forelegs—for antlers in velvet were tender, and an injury to them would result in extensive bleeding; but one came right down upon the watcher, the wind ruffling up the mane at his throat, as he stood boldly at gaze. Then, when less than a hundred yards distant, the wind struck him full, and with a plunge he was off at the gallop.

*　　　*　　　*　　　*　　　*

This was the season when Winter traditionally made his last sortie from the hills, harassing the lambing shepherd with unseasonable snowstorms and hard frosts. No matter that primroses and celandines were now bursting their buds in sheltered

glades on the loch side, that larches were bedecked
with pink flower-tufts, that birches were beginning
to leaf, and thorns in lower glens were a mass of
greenery; nor that at a height of 2,500 feet, in the
stoniest and most desolate of all his corries, the watcher
had already found promise of summer in the crimson
buds and large pink flowers of the purple saxifrage,
creeping over a watercourse. Of no avail that sitting
on the hill above his house, on May morn, he had
marvelled that where before had been an indeterminate brown forest of dead timber, was now a
palest green, billowing canopy of birch woods,
girdling the hill for further than his eye could follow
their course round the loch; or that the green canopy
whispered the plaintive falling melodies of little
warbling birds, just returned in their thousands from
their indomitable voyages to the southernmost bounds
of Africa.

Even while he rejoiced that summer was on its
way, winter mocked him. Three days later a fearful
wind began to blow, that seemed as cold as any that
had raged during the winter storms, and all the next
day and the one after a blizzard of small snow drove
out of the north, striving to shroud the warm soil.
By the fourth morning it had settled to the depth
of an inch on the low ground, while the mountain
barrier bore a mantle almost as white and smooth as
at mid-winter. Long icicles hung from the eaves,
flowers were bowed to the ground, fruit bushes
burnt and shrivelled, the birch canopy seared a dull
autumn yellow.

And just as clear, sunny days at mid-winter and in
March had impelled the stags to climb to the snow-

clad tops, so these rapid changes of temperature in May with a range of as much as sixty degrees between minimum night temperatures, very cold on the tops, and maximum day temperatures, very warm in the glens, resulted in much up and down movement among the deer, now replacing their long, rough and wiry winter coats, reinforced with soft under-fur, with the shorter glossy hair of their summer coats— shedding it wholesale in patches, licking their flanks and bringing away lumps of felted hair with their rasping tongues.

Small herds of hinds came down as low on the moors as at any time during the winter, tamely allowing the watcher to approach to within twenty yards of them, while some of the younger red-coated stags, who had not frequented the wallows, even visited the wood beside his house; and one afternoon a sharp thunderstorm, associated with blinding flashes of forked lightning, severe detonating cracks and a downpour of hail in the form of jagged lumps of ice, brought a small herd of hinds trotting down from the higher moors, almost in panic, to the shelter of some crags by a lochan, though a herd of stags continued to feed, unmoved, on the skyline. Only one of the hinds noticed the watcher standing on the crags, but her fellows took immediate note of her sudden departure, and after pointing their ears forward and looking in the wrong direction for a minute or so, moved off after her.

But if the month of May usually saw the death of winter so, too, it often conquered with the longest and hottest spell of the Highland summer. The stags, still in very poor condition, felt such heat greatly, despite their daily peat bath; and with the thermometer registering seventy or eighty degrees fahrenheit, they might be observed standing lethargically in mid-river in the Glen of Crags too listless to move as the watcher passed by. It might be evening before they would climb as high as 3,500 feet to cool themselves on a snowfield in a hanging corrie.

*   *   *   *   *

It was usually well on into April or, in a late winter, not until May, before the deer opened up their wallows in the peat-hags, which might be high up in the pine forest, though commonly in the middle of a boggy corrie, such as the Heather Corrie, with a long clear field of vision on all sides. They were impelled to open up these wallows by the acute irritation associated with the moult and with the emergence of the warble-fly grubs; while a contributory factor was the irritation of loosening antlers and the urge to get one's head down and thrash among the heather and tussocks. But the actual date of wallowing was governed by the stags' health. The more forward they were in condition, the earlier in the spring they began to shed their winter coats; and one fair evening in the second week of March, in a very early spring, the watcher had caught his breath at the sudden beauty of seven coal-black stags pacing out of the Heather Corrie to join their tawny fellows feeding forward across the bleached moors—magnificent sables in all but name. Such, in certain lights and at a distance of upwards of a mile, were the splendid trappings of a stag fresh from the peat-hags. At closer range he would prove to be a handsome nigger-brown—the colour of a Shetland moorit sheep's lamb.

Two of this herd of seventy stags had already cast their antlers, and would thus have hard antlers clear of velvet as early as the opening week of July. With only six weeks of really hard weather behind them they were in fine fettle, and the leader of the herd was as mad as a March hare, galloping around in small circles, belly almost flat to the ground, plunging away at tangents, digging his antlers into the heather; then chasing the nearest stag for scores of yards, only to break off the pursuit and dash off at full stretch in the opposite direction—to the bewilderment of his immediate fellows, who stood watching until he turned in his tracks again, when they scattered in some alarm. But after some minutes of these high-spirited antics he quietened down, and settled to feed.

Though the hinds tended to use a different type of wallow to the stags, often rolling in clear water, there was no doubt a sufficiently strong solution of peat in this to serve as a soothing lotion. Three or four hinds would wallow together, making quite a sport of it, though hinds could never agree together for long, and the party usually ended in a boxing match.

The wallows would remain open until the middle of June, when, if the weather was favourable, there was a general exodus to the high uplands, where both stags and hinds would roll in pools of water or peat on hot summer days.

But this year, deep tongues of snow, hundreds of yards long, still filled cleft corries down to 2,000 feet

on the third day of June; and with continuous rain
after noon and cloud settling intermittently on the
ridges, the only deer to be seen on the uplands was
one solitary hind, heavy with calf, trotting away
from that little lochan in the central pit of the mosses.
Hers was the strong gait of a frightened deer: head
held erect with ears cupped right forward, knees
high stepping, pointed hooves turned under, with
all the style of a pacer at a trotting match.

It was these few milk hinds, whose habit it was
to calve on these inhospitable uplands, in contrast
to the majority of their fellows who calved in the
higher, but sheltered, portions of their wintering
glens and corries—it was these adventurous spirits,
together with the yeld hinds and older stags, who
were the pioneers of this annual summer exodus to
the high places.

She, as it happened, was not the first calving hind
the watcher had surprised this spring. Four days
earlier a hind had got up from the heather on the
moors near that craggy lochan, to which a herd had
retreated during the thunderstorms, and by the way
she lowered her muzzle to sniff the heather, he was
sure that she had an early calf. He was confirmed
in this belief, when he noted how she stopped four
or five times and looked back. And so she had—but
the calf was still-born.

This was the first time he had observed a hind
actually beside a dead calf, and it recalled to him the
experience of a stalker in a neighbouring forest who
had watched a hind leave a herd feeding in a high
corrie, and trot swiftly down the corrie for a mile.
Then she came to a sudden stop and lowered her

head to the ground, before walking round and round, with head still lowered. Finally she lifted her head and uttered a loud and prolonged wailing bark; then trotted swiftly up the corrie again, not stopping until she reached the herd. She, too, had a dead calf.

However late the spring the low ground was clear of deer before the middle of June; and though the weather continued cold, with frosts on some nights, to the thirteenth, when a westerly gale was blowing on top, the watcher, going his rounds of forest and glen that day, could find only one deer—an old stag feeding, often scratching his jaw, far up the Red Corrie.

Few deer would brave such a day on the actual uplands, and there was abundant evidence of their presence in the glen overnight, with slots everywhere on peaty edges to lochans: but henceforward they would shelter from stormy weather, not in the wintering glens, but in the upper corries and in the deep glens within the mountains, where many of the hinds bore their calves.

The spacious corrie seemed strangely empty, now that the deer's eight months' occupation had ended; but lying in the clean dry heather on the upper edge of the forest, where the pines stood on bright green pedestals of blaeberry—vivid islands among the sea of dull rose-brown heather—the watcher was conscious of the incomparable peace of his hills, as he looked upon the smooth sweep of their giant breasts, whose green-brown slopes enveloped the corrie, and heard the wind sighing through the dry lichenous framework of the stunted pines, on this

light day with heavy galleons of cumulo-nimbus
ever carrying showers from the Atlantic.

And there was that old stag. The watcher had
known him for a long time. He had never carried a
good head, and for twenty years or so had first been
ignored by stalkers, and latterly had eluded them.
During these last years his antlers had diminished in
size and shapeliness year by year, and now his front
teeth were missing and his grinders worn down and
decayed, and he was deaf.

By day he lay up in that jungle of young pines
and belly-high heather in the most inaccessible
retreats of the Black Woods; and there the watcher
had once come upon him sleeping, head turned
back across flank, on his strange couch, which was
the flattened top of one of those huge pine-needle
mounds of the wood-ants, long forsaken by its indus-
trious inhabitants. Its mossy ramp, six feet long and
four feet wide, built up against the base of a small
pine tree, had been worn as smooth as a beaten
earth floor and carpeted with many seasons' cast
hair.

In the summer the old stag fed by himself in one
of the higher corries, plucking the tops of the heather,
in which he lay up during the heat of the day.

In the autumn he took no part in the Rut, and the
watcher had found him idling in the glen, indifferent,
deaf perhaps, to the roaring of his fellows, passing
an hour at a time cautiously rubbing his mis-shapen
antlers up and down the naked bole of an old pine,
barkless from the rubbing of many stags and hinds
through the years; for these old stags experienced
difficulty in ridding their antlers of velvet, especially

when this hardened on the horn in a dry season—
and equal difficulty in shedding their winter coats.

Then he would return to his winter lair in the
forest, from which he would venture forth in the
moonlight, very slowly and stealthily at first, before
breaking into a trot when well clear of the wood, to
raid the hill farmers' corn, still lying out in the stook
in November or December; and later the stacks
themselves, though these might be hard-by the stead-
ing; and the potato clamps, which he pried open
with hoof and antler—surviving somehow, by cun-
ning, displaying much intelligence in negotiating
the fences he could no longer leap, laying his head
along between two wires and manœuvering his
antlers, then getting his forefeet up and forcing his
body through, no matter how taut the wires; while
he varied the localities of his raids from night to
night, baffling the farmer waiting with shotgun.

To have come safely through such a terrible winter
was a remarkable achievement, though in fact
casualties among the herds had been light on the
watcher's ground. Indeed he had found only
twelve dead deer, and three of these had been young
stags in good condition, who had probably died
from gorging too freely on the young grass after
the winter's dry diet. Nevertheless so hard and prolonged a winter would knock a stone or more off the
stags' weight in the autumn, no matter how good the
summer grazing might be.

It was always round about the marshes and along
the burn sides that the dead were to be found in the
spring and early summer—though, less numerously
in these central Highlands than in the watcher's

old home in the mild wet West, despite the fact that
there was ample forest shelter in that country.   It
was not shelter that was the prime essential, but the
presence of extensive tracts of long heather.   Food
in itself, heather also spread a protective covering
over mosses, lichens and berry-plants.   On a deer-
forest, well-timbered, but with little heather, less
than twenty miles south-west of the Eagles' Glen,
it had been reported to the watcher that every burn
held its dead beast, and that 280 dead stags had
been counted this spring.   That, no doubt, was an
exaggerated figure, but it emphasized the possible
mortality in a forest lacking winter feed.

Heather was life to the deer.   Without heather
there could be no red deer, now that the forests
had been felled, and nearly all the low ground
enclosed.

IV

SUMMER

IT was on a fair day in mid-June, with the sun shining brightly from an early hour, that the watcher traversed thirty miles of the uplands between eight in the morning and seven in the evening.

The most delightful season of the mountain year had dawned; for as the hinds bore their calves, so the upland pastures grew green and the few exquisite alpine flowers blossomed: earliest among them the heath, azalea, whose dark olive mats of leaves, ten feet in diameter in some instances, blazed with crimson buds and paler star-flowers.

Over all the mosses and far up in the high corries of the surrounding giants were hundreds of deer. The watcher counted up to 700, and then abandoned himself to the enjoyment of observing this immense gathering, scattered in herds of from twenty to sixty. Some herds of hinds included as many as ten great-antlered stags, for these high summer grazings were a place where the customary conventions of deer society might lapse.

Here and there were smaller groups of five or six hinds, or even just one hind and her yearling. Such a pair would be highly suspicious of the watcher's yellow collie, deeming him perhaps a fox, and would come trotting up for a closer inspection, and linger so long as the watcher remained in the vicinity, the hind stamping a forefoot and yelping at intervals, the yearling blaring. Somewhere near at hand a calf would be lying out: but it was not to be found.

Not until she was three and commonly four years old would a hind bare her first calf. Nor would she necessarily calve regularly every year after that, and the probability was that after a barren season she would bear a stag calf the following summer.

The small spring herds of hinds had begun to break up at the approach of the calving season, as those hinds in calf made away to their traditional calving places, driving off their followers. Thus, it was at this season that those staggies rising three years old ceased to be permanent members of the hind group, wandering off on their own and gradually herding up with other stags, mainly of their own age. But yearlings were not to be driven away in this manner. For them the hinds' chasings and buffetings were a form of play, though somewhat rougher than that to which they were accustomed, when they were bowled over with a brutal dunt in the ribs. It was all very puzzling to these innocents, for one day the hinds would themselves be leaping and wriggling and kicking up their heels, but the next day they would be savage and unfriendly. However, once the calf was born, the nervous yearling was once more accepted as a member of the family.

Abandoning his search for the calf, the watcher continued on down towards the middle of the mosses, and as he did so those herds nearest trotted together, until a magnificent concourse of some 400 deer, mainly stags with half-grown antlers, though sixty great heads among them, were massed together. Almost, it seemed to him, that he had been transported back over the centuries and was witnessing a *tainchel* through some narrow pass—such as that deep canyon on the far side of the mosses, into which, 300 years before his day, several hundred Highlanders, rising before dawn and scattering seven or ten miles through the forests around the uplands, had been wont to drive herds of hundreds of deer, to be shot at with long bows and arquebuses, and pulled down by greyhounds.

As the deer ran together before him, so there was a great din of hinds barking, yearlings blaring, and calves bleating. Indeed he was not at all sure that he did not hear a stag roar. It was not impossible: hummels had been known to roar as early as July. And as he traversed over the mosses, bound for the high ridge in the east, seen on his way by pairs of golden plover standing watchful with plaintive piping each on his knoll, either side the faint trail of the old bridle-path, so the great herd streamed, protesting, before him, making their way to a favourite corrie high up on the sweep of that long rounded hill forming the southern barrier to the mosses.

And there was no other man on the hill. Just the watcher and the deer in this mountain sanctuary: this other world, still as it was on the first day, where man had never ploughed a furrow, felled a tree, or built a stone-dyke, though 150 years agone the herdsmen and herd girls—Margaret was one—had fashioned for their shelter on these summer pastures little stone bothies roofed with turf sods: hardy folk.

By ten o'clock he had crossed the four mile west-east span of the mosses and had come up against a ruined cairn, which marked the scene of a strange tragedy, some ninety years earlier, when a stalker, following a wounded stag for six miles up that long

Glen of the Tainchel, which was the main deer high-
way from the eastern glens up onto the mosses, had
finally come up with it at this point; but as it was
difficult to bring a stalking pony through the deep
gorge, he had attempted to drive the stag down into
the gorge, and hit it on the haunch with his loaded
rifle . . . His companions had found him lying dead
across the stag's body, shot through the heart.

And here it was, at no great distance from the cairn,
that, a few hours earlier, a hind had dropped her calf
on a little flat of grass beside a shallow stream, after
her restless night of labour, during which she had
continually risen, bellowing softly, from her calving
place, to walk around for a little, head held low,
before returning to lie down again; though when the
calf was born she was on her feet.

Now, hardly yet dry, the calf lay curled up with its
smooth head turned back across outstretched forelegs,
yellow hooves still doubled under. Its large opaque
bluish-brown eyes were open, its nose still crinkled
and unformed, pulsing in and out intermittently as it
breathed.

Not yet was it tainted with fear of man. It did not
stir, nor even blink, while the watcher sat beside it,
stroking it with a bunch of fir-club fingers, not wishing
to leave his scent too strong upon its sleek brown
body, so neatly dappled with tufts of white hair:
what time its dam stood hesitant, sixty or seventy
yards distant, neither approaching nor retreating.

It was commonly believed by stalkers that for the
first few days after a calf's birth it was visited and
suckled by the hind only twice a day, morning and
evening, and that at the end of this period—variously

estimated at from two to seven days—it was strong
enough to run with the hinds and her followers.

Very probably this was so when the calf was dropped
in the long heather of glen or corrie, or, as sometimes
happened, actually among the long grass in a marshy
meadow beside a shooting lodge—though, unless the
stalker stayed watching all through the twilight
northern night, how was it known that the hind did
not stay with the calf during the night? But, even
if this were true of glen calves—and all the evidence
was that the hind was seldom so far away that she
could not run to the calf's assistance were it attacked
by fox or eagle—it was a routine that did not apply
to these mountain babies, whose mothers were always
somewhere in their vicinity, during the hours of
daylight, if not at night.

Lying out on bare stony flat or grassy sward, during
this initial period of helplessness, the mountain calf
was without cover to conceal it from fox or cat. One
defence lay in its probable lack of scent, quite un-
detectable so far as the watcher was concerned, though
not necessarily so to a keen-nosed fox. Foxes, however,
were not numerous on these barren uplands, where
there were no rabbits, rarely a hare, and only a score
or two of nesting ptarmigan. Foxes, with cubs to
feed at this season, were much more of a menace to
calves born in the glens, though they did not stand
upon the order of their going if the hind came charging
up with those murderous sharp hooves of hers.

The fierce wild-cats, too, preferred the wooded
crags high up in rabbit-haunted glens, though one
autumn day the watcher had surprised one of these
huge tabbies sunning himself at noon on a rocky shelf

2,000 feet up the bare mountainside, and very much at his ease—front paws together, back legs sprawled sideways, rounded black-ringed tail twitching spasmodically. That summer the den in the ancient birch forest below had housed six kittens and, among a variety of game, no fewer that twenty oystercatchers. These, however, had not proved acceptable to the kittens, and were almost untouched; but their presence provided an unexpected clue to a wild-cat's mobility, for there were not twenty pairs of oystercatchers nesting throughout the glen's ten miles.

The calf's second defence lay in its inconspicuousness; for at a distance of thirty paces its pale mole-brown body was almost invisible to a man's eye. Though who should say what was hidden from the piercing eye of a hunting eagle? But then, again, it was mainly the young eagles who hunted the uplands during the summer months, preying on ptarmigan. The old eagles quartered rabbits and hares in the wilder glens and on the high moorlands as food for their eaglets. 100 years ago, perhaps, when predators of all kinds abounded, eagles might have taken, probably did take, more deer calves, and even attacked full-grown hinds or stags on occasions; but it was now several years since the watcher had witnessed an eagle taking a calf, and that had been in his old home in the West.

On one occasion a hind had been feeding at some distance from her calf, and though she had rushed up, she was too late to prevent the great bird carrying off the calf in his fearful talons. Despite his seven-feet wing-span, however, the eagle found the calf a heavy burden, and unable to gain height, dropped it after flying a few· score yards. On a second

attempt, however, he was more successful, and
laboured away with the new born calf over the hill.

On another occasion an eagle had dropped on,
or almost on, to the back of a big calf running with
the herd; but in this instance the hind was as scared
as her calf and did not stop to savage the eagle. On
the watcher running up, however, the eagle swooped
up and the calf galloped safely after the herd.

*   *   *   *   *

"No, little chap, you have little to fear up here,"
said the watcher, voicing his own thoughts and ad-
dressing his calf, "And you are much safer than you
would be down in the glen. No other man will ever
handle you—alive; but strong you must be, to withstand the cutting wind and lashing rain, the arctic
cold and dank swirling cloud of these desolate heights,
with no warm bed of heather or bracken to shelter
you; and I know that you see your mother much
more often than twice a day, and that she shelters you
from the worst of the weather; but does she stay with
you on those nights of pitchy blackness, when the
blue-green lightning glimmers around the hills from
second to second, and flickers from crag to crag?
You are one of the lucky ones, born in the early
morning of this rare day of mountain summer."

And indeed it was only once or twice in a season
that the watcher could enjoy such a sight as was to
be seen from his seat near the cairn, with a light
breeze to temper the heat of the sun, which was very
much fiercer on the tops than in the glens. True,
the deer were in such poor condition that they were
as lean as rakes except for their rotund swollen bellies;

and, with their rumps cut away to nothing, it was the projecting hocks of those immensely long hind legs that were their most prominent back feature. Moreover, both hinds and yearlings were casting their coats in a deplorable manner, loose hair standing up in unkempt tufts; while those who had moulted on neck and rump bore the appearance of wearing woollen jerkins. But, if they were still a long way from being in prime condition, their step was as strong and springy as ever. They stepped like racehorses in the ring, so thin and finely drawn their frames, so long of leg, while the pale interiors of their long ears, glinting in the sun, created the illusion of antlers.

It was too early yet in the season for flies or other insects to trouble them, nor were there blood-sucking ticks anywhere in this stony well-drained country. For a few blessed days they were free from pests. Above all, they were full fed: winter's hardships past. To-morrow did not enter into their world . . . or did it? Why did the hinds seek out traditional calving places, if they had no awareness of the future? And what about those downward migrations from the hills when they smelt snow?

Already the watcher's disturbing intrusion had been forgotten. Though reclining in full view, he had become an accepted feature of the uplands, as harmless as that ancient tumbled cairn. A high stony flat on the far side of the stream was crowded with hinds basking in the sun, their calves stretched out luxuriously beside them, while other calves scampered from hind to hind, bleating squeakily, seeking their own mothers, who lowed softly to them. One calf was sucking. Its year-old sister thought

that she would like a drink too, but instead of looking
for this on the hind's free side, she deliberately butted
the calf in the rump; but the latter was not going to
be deprived of its drink, and refused to give way to
the yearling, even when butted a second time. The
hind ignored this byplay, and on the yearling returning, after the calf had drunk its fill, placidly allowed it
to drink also; though most hinds only allowed yearlings
to muzzle in when the calf was actually sucking.

Life assuredly was good on this fair summer day,
and soon all the calves were on their feet and playing
like lambs, six or seven suddenly darting from their
mothers' sides, to chase together, racing up and down
and round about, leaping over the rocks, no matter
how insignificant, and sometimes tumbling on their
noses, reversing and going off at tangents, then racing
back to their mothers for a refresher—only to break
away again, one attracting another, converging this
time on a little knoll, which one calf would mount,
followed by the others, when there was a general
helter-skelter down again.

Never had the watcher been conscious of greater
serenity of spirit as he sat beside his calf, watching
these innocent sports, and it was with reluctance that
he tore himself away, but he wished to discover how
high the deer were feeding on this ideal day; and only
when he actually rose and left the calf did its mother
finally trot away, while at a bark from one old hind
all the calves ran to their mothers.

A little higher up the hill he disturbed another
calf—a bigger, ruddier-coated one—which trotted
away very swiftly over broken ground littered with
tumbled rocks, while its mother and elder sister, who

had been feeding at a distance, cantered off in the opposite direction.

And as he climbed the hill, halting often to look down upon the pleasant scene, he perceived that the first hind had already returned to her calf and was nosing it thoroughly, her maternal instinct dominant to her fear of man's hated scent.

It was a climb of more than a thousand feet up the long steep corrie to the high ridge. In the lower parts of the corrie grey screes reached down from either slope into the pale mountain pastures and the greening edges of a watercourse, whose shallow winding channel was paved with slabs and clumps of moss: green, yellow and brown, and grotesque blood-coloured mosses of every lurid shade of red and purple, on which craneflies danced on their tails, depositing their eggs. But, at 3,500 feet, he passed into the true alpine zone of steep moraines of grey or pink granite blocks and boulders, stained green with the neatly scrawled whorls of map-lichen, or blackened with cushion-moss, which the deer found edible in the autumn. Clumps of hard-fern were wedged into crevices among the rocks.

To this corrie, for as many years as the watcher had known the uplands, a pair of snow-buntings—loneliest bird of Scottish mountains—had returned every June to rear their young in crannies among the boulders, and many the time he had been startled, as to-day, by the sudden surprising burst of lark-like melody thrown into the silent corrie by the gorgeous black and white cock-bird, as he flitted from one rock to another or floated across the corrie on outspread wings,

He had known a hind to drop her calf on a grassy patch on the lower edge of the boulders in this high corrie.   Surely no red deer calves had ever been born higher.

At the head of the corrie he stepped out onto the very roof of the Highlands, onto an immense flat of gravel, 500 acres in extent, and more than 4,000 feet above sea-level. Though so early in the summer, this flat of shifting granite grit was already a beautiful rock-garden of moss campion, whose cushions of deepest china-pink reached out wherever sedges and fringe-moss failed. So densely massed the flowerlets, they concealed the green cushions beneath.

On either side the flat shelved down from solid fields of snow to a depression of many bubbling springs and the narrow green of a pebble-clear burn, where sedges and coarse grasses were already growing strongly. He was not surprised to find a group of seven hinds, with three calves, couched and feeding along the watercourse. And here, too, on the third day of August one summer he had found a mountain hare's leveret which, with its large and prominent brown eyes and not very long ears, its drab-brown curly coat, with only a little smoke-blue fur around the tail, resembled the brown hare of the lowlands much more closely than did its parents.

At the far end of the flat the stream cascaded through a cutting in the broad cornice of snow, which still formed a thick frieze to the sphinx-like crags falling away sheer to an immense corrie, some 2,000 feet deep, seamed with burns and a chaos of fallen rocks. Far down in this devil's cauldron, already shaded from the noonday sun, two hinds were feeding.

This was a safe, though savage refuge for their calves; but for some unknown reason deer did not now feed in this sanctuary, with its near-perpetual snowfields, as numerously as they had done fifty years before.

Trudging through the heavy gravel, he almost trod on a ptarmigan brooding her young, who scattered when she burst into activity, shuffling her wings. Though only a few hours old, the three chicks ran swiftly, all ways, over the shingle, balancing with diminutive wing-arms outspread.

Stooping down, he placed one on the palm of his hand. What an exquisite little mite it was in its variegated gold and olive down, laced with brown threads, and golden-haired even on legs and feet. Yet it was most conspicuous against the patch of black and grey shingle, on which it had crouched, in contrast to its mother who, walking quietly around in her blackish-grey plumage, blended perfectly with her background.

Toiling on up to the peak, a couple of hundred feet above the flat, the watcher passed into a lunar world devoid of all plant-life—a pyramid of flat granite slabs and boulders, piled one upon another so closely that there was only space to walk from one rocking slab to another. Only ptarmigan, belching sacrilegiously, visited this sterile peak, from whence the watcher could look over seventy miles of range upon range of deer hills to the western ocean and fifty miles to the northern firth.

When, three hours later, he came down again from that desolation of cosmic disintegration to the serene world of the deer, he found that his calf, though still curled in the same posture, had turned round. It would change its bed several times, before finally quitting it for good. Already it was probing the mystery of existence: for in its mouth was a spray of tormentil; but it was still unafraid.

*   *   *   *   *

Midsummer's interlude was followed by a spell of wet and windy weather, with cold cloud lying on the 3,000-foot ridges for long periods. Some of the stags came down from the uplands again, and herds of big stags twenty strong, their antlers, thickened with velvet, doubly magnificent, raided the crops of outlying farms in the early morning; while nearly every evening nine or ten stags, big and small, would appear over the brow of the hill above the watcher's house, and sit calmly enjoying the evening breeze, which dispelled the midges.

They might rest there for two hours or even longer, until the setting sun was lipping the western fells. Only then would they rise, one by one, and draw leisurely down the face of the hill in twos and threes along the burn-side, taking a bite here and a bite there as they went, but ever on the move.

If stags could see thus far, they might have discerned other stags from a western forest also enjoying the evening breeze on the summit crest of a great hill on the far side of the strath, eight miles distant and 1,500 feet above a stalker's white cottage; but these stags from east and west would never meet, not even during the Rut, for a railway and two main roads lay between them.

Did stags have thoughts, couched on these high places, with that splendid prospect over the broad

strath spread out before them, or did they just cud
in cervine vacancy? No doubt they were more
appreciative of the taste, than of the colour, of grass
but how the strath had changed since those terrible
winter evenings when eager heads had appeared
over the brow of that hill!

So vivid a green was the grass now that it was
almost too bright for eyes so long accustomed to the
bleached yellows and whites, dead browns and
colourless greys of the sapless Highland winter and
spring. And there was the green, too, of larches
spiring from the yet brown alder-groves; and, always,
the black-green pinewoods, whose colour had been
so precious through the long naked winter. Within
the birch woods were green slopes of bluebells and
green masses of ferns.

It was good to be alive on those mild evenings,
sweet with the fragrance of birch leaves and drowsy
with the musk of rowan flowers, when swallows skim-
med the water-meadows, and burnished copper
redstarts, with powdered silver brows and jet, damask
cheeks, darted down to pools of sunlight chequering
the shadowy road through the pinewoods; to lie on a
mossy bank in one of the little wood parks and hear a
cuckoo shout a hundred times without a pause. Three
cuckoos calling in harmony, roused the wood-owls
to hoot sleepily; while ever in the background was
the elusive laughter of warblers and the sweet, sane
bell-notes of titmice, the merry jingoes of siskins,
swinging like little gold parrots from pine-cones, and
the resonant drumming of woodpeckers, black and
white and scarlet.

A startlingly shiny black nose poked through a

briar bush and was followed by the rough-pearled horns of a roe-buck; but something startled him, and he bounded up the steep hanger of the wood, pausing once to bark and stamp a slender steel foreleg. Glossy in shaggy summer coat, he was as dark a red as a polished pine limb.

Noticing some little heaps of cone flakes, the watcher looked up to see a red squirrel sleeping along a pine branch. With head and tufted ears couched on paws, and bushy tail curled over back and projecting an inch in front of its face, it resembled a large hairy fir-cone.

And then there was another squirrel, nibbling at a larch cone, which it turned round and round with its paws with remarkable rapidity, before quickly throwing it down. Then, sitting forward on the branch it studied the watcher.

A scrabbling of claws in the momentary stillness, and a third squirrel whisked up a rough-barked pine. And then there were five! Three squirrels a-chasing and there was a blaze of colour, as, each on another's tail, they slithered round and round and up and down the pine bole, squeaking excitedly, so swiftly that the watcher's impression was of a whirling red-gold catherine-wheel.

Suddenly, spontaneously, all three interrupted their erratic convolutions and froze to the trunk, hanging head downwards in luxurious abandon the length of their widely parted hind-legs, fore-paws hanging free, as if set-pinned; while their fine-haired tails lay flush with the bark, or wagged furiously from side to side.

For several minutes the three maintained absolute immobility, with prominent round black eyes fixed

upon the watcher, though one still held a large cone
in its mouth; and then, as suddenly, and spontaneously
they flashed into lightning activity.

One scrabbled up the trunk with extraordinary
swiftness, mainly on its sun-less side away from the
watcher, to the very top of the tree; then out along
the bending clusters of needles, pirouetting upon the
slenderest twigs with airy grace and agility, before
leaping far out to another tree-top, with a motion so
effortless that it appeared to the watcher merely a
leisurely removal from one place to another, yet so
swift in fact that his eye followed the acrobat with
difficulty; and hardly had the squirrel seemed to
alight, swaying on the outer twigs, before it was
twisting half out into space again, peering for a cone.
Tearing one off with filed teeth, it swung back to a
securer perch on the very tip of the tree; and then
scampered down the trunk: to be away in a flash,
bounding sinuously over the pine-needles, almost as if
a stoat, to bury the cone at the base of another tree;
but having scratched a hole, it filled it with needles
and placed the cone on top! Then it returned to
sit on a nearby log and study the watcher once more
with those beady black eyes.

Suddenly its mate appeared . . . Another scampering
to the top of the tree, and a shower of cone flakes
falling upon the watcher's upturned face. Then down
came one again, to squat on a projecting snag, only
six feet from the watcher, in favourite squirrel attitude
sitting back against the trunk, chewing a cone, with
fluffy tail waving from side to side in the breeze—
only to hurl the cone away, with that febrile ir-
responsibility of all squirrel actions, to which it was

provoked from minute to minute, scratching its head, stamping with hind or fore feet, wagging its tail excitedly, chattering with angry *choc-choc-choc*.

*　　*　　*　　*　　*

For the deer, however, life was no couch of roses. There was food a'plenty now, but a new season of insect pests had begun. Midges tormented them in all sheltered places and even on the lower hills, and were torture to the stags in velvet, whose antlers were too tender to suffer vigorous rubbing or scratching. The most a stag could do was to scrape his antlers very gently against a tree, or scratch them tentatively with a hind hoof. Only on the windy uplands could the deer find relief from these minute pests; but even that sanctuary had been invaded by a more formidable if less numerous pest; as the watcher discovered, when on a fair morning towards the end of June he breasted the stalker's path to the uplands, to the accompaniment of the ubiquitous pipits' tinkling songs.

The steep corries bisecting the mountain barrier still contained long stockings of snow, filling them almost from top to bottom; and one of these snowfields —now in sun, now in shade on a warm morning— presented an extraordinary sight, being dotted for most of its length with stags. As many as sixty could be seen on it at one time, with others continually coming on to it from their feeding places on the adjacent slopes, to spend a few minutes standing or couched on the snow.

Half an hour later, when the gully was sunlit, the watcher was close enough to see that every now and again a stag would make a little run across the snow;

while one mighty beast—one of the few with full antlers—standing four-square and relaxed, heavy in front, belly sagging a little with hind legs stretched back slightly, would plunge his muzzle into the snow from time to time.

It was the nostril-fly, a large black and yellow, bee-like insect, which was troubling the deer, hovering over their muzzles and ejecting drops of fluid containing larvae into their nostrils—an attention to which they invariably objected strongly and unmistakably. The larvae would attach themselves to the membranes of the deer's nasal cavities, where they would remain with only local movements, until sneezed out by the deer the following May.

Far above the stags, on the big snowfield in the cleft just below the summit, a hind and her yearling were standing motionless, casting their shadows on the snow; and when they did eventually walk up to feed on the green above, the yearling quickly came cantering back to put its nose close to the snow, and to couch for a minute or two, before running up after its dam, who had fed over the skyline.

Deer understood snow, and four or five tracks crossed the depressed flange of the snowfield, though this was now distinctly "hinged" towards the bottom. Not once in a generation was a herd of deer trapped by an avalanche. It was indeed nearly 50 years since a herd of twenty-three stags and hinds had been overwhelmed by an avalanche in the Eagles' Glen.

Though the bothie on the summit was still three-quarters buried in snow, only a sparse network of snowfields, some broad and deep, lingered in the watercourses and shallower corries of the mosses. At first sight the vast expanse of upland seemed empty, but as his eyes began to register light and shade, hill and flat, the watcher became aware that the deer were scattered widely over it in small herds. A few stags, indeed, were sitting on a small patch of snow in a peat-hag immediately below him, while another small herd could be descried on a big snowfield at a height of 3,500 feet.

It was at two o'clock, when he had gone down to the lochan, beneath whose wintry surface a glaucous-green undershelf of frozen snow still projected from a broad snowfield on the western bank, that the watcher noticed that a score of hinds were feeding on that high flat south of the cairn near which he had found the calf, and observed with pleasure that one of their number was licking the head, and more especially the ears, of a tottery calf. A cross-wind was blowing, but as there was a Y of interrogation on the edge of the hill, 300 yards distant, he sat himself down, hoping that the hinds would feed away from him, but prepared for a long wait.

One of the uplands' few skylarks was singing hardby; but when it fell to earth the mountain silence was heightened by the distant surge of waterfalls and the occasional tinkle of a pipit or buzz of fly, until three golden plover flighted yodelling overhead and two little dunlin glided over the peat-hags, "reeling" persistently. Reclining on the slope of the hill, the watcher idly examined the plants to hand. Curious that the minute, pale crimson flowers of the crowberry should lie in the axils of their polished dull-green leaf-stems.

From time to time the calf's mother, feeding at

the edge of the herd, would raise her head and, pointing her ears upwind, gaze back at the calf now lying down some scores of yards distant. There were many small chivyings among the feeding herd, the yearlings often running through their fellows, causing the hinds to lay back their ears angrily, and once one reared up to box briefly. Occasionally an older hind would lift her head—very mare-like, as she stood chewing, ears half-lop.

Three-quarters of an hour elapsed, and the hinds were still grazing down the opposite slope towards him. It was clearly not going to be possible to approach the calf without disturbing them, so getting up the watcher strolled leisurely across their front, gradually narrowing the 250 yards gap between them and himself by half. The breeze was now blowing from behind the hinds and, though bunching together, they did not retreat during this operation, which lasted for some minutes; and only finally trotted away over the rim of the flat in the direction of the calf, when he was halfway up its steep fall.

Ten minutes later he sighted them again, already settling down to the all-important business of feeding. They had only removed a hundred yards. The calf was now half-walking, half crawling on the "pasterns" of doubled under hooves in a pathetic, wounded sort of way, a pace or two behind its dam, who kept looking round at it solicitously.

What determined little creatures these red deer calves were! Long before they could run with their mothers, they would hobble and shuffle over the roughest ground in this manner, and would probably do so when less than a day old, for a calf could totter to its feet within a few minutes of birth, stilt-like front legs widely straddled.

On sighting the watcher the hind tapped the calf gently with her hoof and pressed it down with her muzzle. Again the hinds bunched and stood contemplating him, as he made a direct approach to within seventy-five yards of them, before all, including the dam, trotted away over the east side of the flat. Yet, six months back in the hind-shooting season, these same hinds would have run from him when he was 400 or 500 yards distant.

Shortly after they had made off, a young hind appeared over the south edge of the flat, with a dappled calf at foot. For a full minute, the hind stared at the watcher, before wheeling round the way she had come with the calf running hard at her side. It was always something of a mystery how these diminutive calves, less than a week old, could keep pace with a herd of hinds, even when the latter were cantering.

The baby calf he found couched in a little hollow among some small rocks imbedded in the soft woolly fringe-moss, his head resting comfortably on one such flat rock. Fawnish-brown he was, speckled with white flecks on back, sides and haunches, with a thin black stripe down the length of his spine from his prominent dark-brown poll, still damp-streaked from the rasp of his mother's tongue, rough as a cat's, to his woolly copper-coloured tail with its whitish surround. His face and nose were a dark mouse-brown, with ears, laid back tightly against his head, of a lighter colour: his muzzle white and cheeks pale fawn: while the lashes of his dark-brown eyes were

an inch in length. Generations of breeding perfection
were revealed in every line of his long-legged body.

Once again, the watcher sat down beside this
newcomer to his herds and wondered about his
destiny, born 3,010 feet above sea-level on this stony
plateau ringed round by giant hills. It would have
been peculiarly satisfying to have marked him in
some way, to have established his individuality for
life. Like the other calf he remained motionless,
though shivering a little when the watcher stroked
him with a handful of fir-moss, crinkling his nose
as he breathed.

Many stalkers had reported calves screaming like
hares when handled, even to the extent of actually
calling up their mothers to the attack. The watcher,
on the contrary, had never known any deer-calf he
had handled to utter a sound, and drew the obvious
conclusion that such calves had been roughly treated.

When he left the calf, after a quarter of an hour,
he found that the hinds had travelled 500 yards, and
were now climbing the lower slopes of the great hill
above the Glen of the Tainchel, feeding as they climbed.
Two hinds with yearlings, however, were standing
watching at the bottom of the hill. One hind, no
doubt was the calf's mother, while the other probably
also had a calf lying out on or near the flat.

It was a further proof of the traditional nature of
the calving places that, to the watcher's knowledge,
calves had always been born on that stony flat, and
on the grassy banks below, for the past thirty years.
With its fir-club moss, mats of crowberry and bunches
of yellowish-white or tender green shoots of the
stag's-horn lichen, this flat was essentially a hind

preserve.   Stags were seldom to be seen grazing on it.

Another type of upland calving place much favoured by the hinds was that almost inaccessible corrie of the purple saxifrage on the home side of the mosses; for just before opening out onto the mosses this corrie branched to form a large amphitheatre, a delightful green corrie whose steep walls sheltered its snug sanctuary from all winds.

* * * * *

After the spell of unfavourable weather the deer were by no means at full strength on the uplands, and thus far the watcher had encountered only some 200 stags and fewer than 100 hinds.   The day was perfect.   Such rare days could not be wasted.   Instead, therefore, of staying up on the mosses, he decided to turn away from home and discover what deer there were in the great glen that penetrated them from the south, beside the Hill of Calves.   So at four o'clock he slithered cautiously down its steep snowfields into the deep gorge, while five wolf-like stags gazed down on him in apparent astonishment from the lip of the opposite siding 500 feet above.   It was twenty-five miles home this way, but it was a decision he was never to regret.

His way down the five miles of this glen lay by narrow deer trails, athwart broken and boggy slopes on either side a rocky stream of numerous falls, and three-quarters of an hour passed before he saw deer again—two herds, each of some fifty-five stags, couched or feeding on the luxuriantly green, south-facing walls of two connecting punch-bowl corries beneath those southern heights of the uplands, where the biggest stags were always to be seen, with this choice sanctuary open to them, once the snow cornices had melted; while on the other side of the stream a big stag was standing out, like an ibex, on some broken crags. Stags would venture down the most perilous precipices in pursuit of some moss or berry plant they craved.

A quarter of an hour later he suddenly rounded a corner onto a beautiful green strip at the edge of the river. Four hinds were feeding at the far end of this pleasance, which was some 150 yards long and 40 yards wide. To his annoyance they lifted their heads and saw him before he had realised that the green was occupied; but it was with reluctance that they climbed a little way up the heather braes fringing this choice pasture of long grass. Moreover, above them on the high moors, half a mile distant, was another small herd of twelve hinds with two calves. On the chance that something interesting might mature, he sat down on the edge of a hollow to refuel with a sandwich or two and the last of his flask of tea, while above the long line of crags cresting the hill two young eagles soared against the storm-clouds.

Though the four hinds had definitely seen him, they had evidently not defined him as an actively dangerous object, even at so short a range. It was, after all, four months since the hind shooting season had closed. They might never have seen a man, since they had gone up from their winter grazings in the Pass of the Crags (where he had watched them in the ancient pinewood in that March blizzard) to the wild waste of moors and uplands above this most inaccessible pasturage. However that might be, they now, rather than suspecting him, were gazing intently at a herd of sixteen stags filing up the hill and over its crest on the other side of the stream; and he was gratified to note that the other herd of hinds had not observed the suspicious movements either of their fellows or of the stags, and were plunging eagerly down the heathery braes river-wards. To be sure, they stopped frequently, to gaze and sniff the breeze very briefly; but these perfunctory precautions would have availed them nought had the watcher been a poacher. They were too eager to begin their evening feed on the grassy flat; and within half an hour of his opening up the green, they were down and feeding greedily. What was more, the other four hinds had, to his astonishment, already forgotten, after so short an interval, the immediate cause of their leaving the green, and were also turning down to join their companions.

Avid for this fresh grass, the sixteen hinds grazed forward steadily, almost quickly, up the flat towards him. They were in notably better condition than their fellows on the uplands.

Why was it, he wondered, that deer visited such places only in the early morning and evening? The mountain sheep went up to rest at night: the deer came *down* to feed, just as in the old days they had come out of the forest to feed at this hour. Fewer midges, clegs and mosquitoes at such hours certainly. But was it possible also that they were aware that during the midday hours of bright sunshine their reddish forms were most conspicuous against a bright green background? It seemed unlikely. Yet it was a fact that deer feeding on green hills favoured rocky and heathery ground during the heat of the day, and might be found in such terrain day after day in June —except, of course, on the uplands, where there was no shade. The dominant reason, however, was probably that low ground was associated with the presence of human beings. This implied, again, that deer remembered the past; and if a memory of the past, why not an awareness of the future?

But this was no time for such debate. This evening the grass was very good, and more ill-tempered jealousy was displayed than he was accustomed to observe among hinds feeding, with many small chivyings: one striking another with a fore-foot, two rearing up and snapping, grinding their teeth viciously, as they drew their faces aside, while the two with calves would not allow the other's calf near their own, muzzling it away, though not actually biting it; for one calf was continually losing its mother, when it stopped and pretended to graze.

By the time that the hinds had fed halfway up the green to within seventy-five yards of the watcher, the latter began to feel embarrassed, for seventy-five yards was a very small distance indeed when the objects in case were as large as a deer or, for that matter, a man. Conventions demanded that at least he should stop eating and drinking, and sit back motionless; though even so he was still in full view of, and on a level with, the bowed heads of the advancing hinds, who proceeded steadily forward— to within fifty yards, then thirty-five yards.

At this range one hind twice looked directly at the watcher, who was sitting broadside on with his legs stretched out in front of him. Guiltily he put down a last sandwich and "froze": but the hind resumed feed-

ing after only a second's gaze. The merest suspicion
that something was not as it should be must have
passed from eye to brain, but was rejected by the latter.

Five yards closer, the breeze blowing across their
front; and now two hinds stared briefly at an object
that was evidently not quite familiar to them in this
traditional feeding place. Green and grey, fawn and
brown were its colours: probably all different shades
of grey to the hinds, though it was sad to think that
that beautiful grass was not green to them, and that
the blue skies over the uplands were always grey. At
intervals two bright discs were added, when the watcher raised his binoculars very slowly.

At seventy-five feet, when he could hear them
tearing up the grass and the click of grating teeth, a
pipit uttered a loud *peep-peep-peep*. Never, he was sure,
had he heard such a noisy pipit, and six heads were
instantly raised, despite the fact that this was a bird call
with which they were as well acquainted as the becking
of grouse. The heads were up for a little longer
this time—long working jaws in strong profile —but
all eventually went down again to that excellent grass.

He was always to regret that at this point the
rocky hollow in which he was sitting should have
forced the leading hinds to change direction slightly
and feed across his front—at which move the calves
sat down, dark little figures almost hidden in the grass,
except for their neat little heads, black noses and
pointed ears.

The nearest hinds were now only sixty feet distant,
directly beyond the watcher's feet, and in order to
obtain a full view of them over the raised coping of
the hollow, he had no alternative but to raise himself

a little; but this slight movement attracted the attention of the oldest hind, who fixed her eyes on him,
while he stared back at her without batting an eyelid.

She really was a ludicrous old hag, with her protruberant, short-sighted brown eyes sunken in the
rounded skeletonal cavities of her wasted pale-grey
face. She was very old, twenty or twenty-five years
maybe, perhaps too old to bear another calf, and from
all appearances most ill-tempered. It was difficult
to credit that she had once been a dainty calf.

For three or four minutes grandma and watcher
stared at one another fixedly. Several times he
blinked, chuckling silently at a memory of an old
fable that a wild beast could not withstand the human
eye, and of the stalker's lore that a deer was frightened
by the slight movements of a man's eye at any lesser
distance than fifty yards.

But finally the old lady was satisfied that he was
definitely not a normal property of this feeding place.
She gave a single hoarse bark. This brought the
calves to their feet, and the hinds moved off in a bunch;
though after trotting only a few yards, Herself, in the
rear, lingered for a second quiz with those puzzled,
bespectacled eyes.

When seventy yards up the brae, the herd stopped,
and from that range stood looking down at the
watcher for the next quarter of an hour, Herself
uttering her single warning bark at long intervals,
while he finished his meal and glassed them frequently.
Not until he got up and walked around stiffly did
they finally get going, the two hinds with calves
leading. And now they really were disturbed at this
unprecedented encounter in their sanctuary. For a

mile or more they trotted along the skyline ahead of the watcher, before disappearing. He had not known deer to run so far from him before, and regretted having broken their evening peace in this delightful place; but perhaps they would have forgotten their experience by the next evening. Seldom had he spent a more enjoyable hour and a half.

In all, there were 140 stags in this glen and thirty hinds; but of the 120 hinds he had seen during the course of the day only four or five had calves, though it was now the peak of the calving season. With the hinds short of milk, after the long winter, many of the calves had died.

And so homeward, down into the Glen of Crags, along the moor path high above the deep white gorge of the river, with its dark brown pools where salmon lay three tiers deep, and down the crumbling cliff track into the ancient pinewood in the pass, where mountain ousels piped forlornly and the peregrine's eyasses screamed from a well-whitened eyrie on the wall of crags, as the falcon twirled down to an overhanging rock.

This was a glen of flowers, and the clammy loam of dripping chasms was gay with sprays of the yellow saxifrage, whose bright yellow petals, exquisitely dusted with orange dots, were set off by palest green sepals. The herb-like wood-sage was here, too, and the pink and green flowers of the mountain sorrel, the curious purple and orange drooping cups of the water-avens, and the graceful tri-fronded fern.

In a grassy glade among the pines and junipers the fairy figure of a yearling roe stood poised with one forefoot raised.

Homeward through the cuckoo-loud glen at sunset, when six young stags came out of the pine forest below the Red Corrie, to canter into the gloaming.

*   *   *   *   *

By July, when the scars of old muir burnings had been painted over by pink sweeps of cross-leaved heather, and gravel scalds on brae faces were empurpled with bell-heather, most of the hinds had calved, and more had gone up on to the uplands or across them into the glens, while the younger stags had moved up out of the lower corries a week earlier.

At long last the brief mountain summer had come to the uplands.

Down the watercourses, among the peat-hags and rocky outcrops, and on the shelving walls of the high corries, were smooth green swards, a little bleached as yet, while boggier flats were gay with spotted orchises, with here and there purple butterworts and pale blue marsh-violets. Along the banks of the burns luxuriant with thick green clumps of golden saxifrage, were alpine willowherb and here and there the exquisite star-saxifrage, whose fragile white star-flowers branched delicately from slender reddish-green stems. In drier places were white cloudberry flowers and the pale yellow trumpets of cow-wheat, while the pink lanterns of the bearberry had now been replaced by the cowberry's white bells. Dwarf eyebright, simulating white heather, and the minute white cruciforms of honey-scented heath-bedstraw laced the short herbage in extraordinary profusion to a height of over 3,500 feet.

Such was the scene, when in the warmest weather

he could remember on the uplands, the watcher passed a day and a night with the deer at mid-month, traversing all the mosses and the peaks and ridges of their surrounding giants. It was only on these peerlessly fine days that he could be certain of finding large numbers of deer on the uplands. On anything less perfect they might, or they might not be up there, and there was no accounting for their presence. There was no such event as the deer going up to the tops to stay. If the weather was changeable, theirs was a daily, not a monthly, up and down movement.

There was yet an hour to go to noon, when, resting on the western escarpment after the arduous climb, he perceived that the deer were indeed at full strength on their summer pastures. For almost a mile across the mosses and up on to the southern heights, over above the Deep Glen wherein he had experienced that memorable encounter with the sixteen hinds, straggled an immense concourse of deer. The high ground in particular was "black" with the backs and heads of resting stags. In this single loosely-knit herd there were more than 500 deer.

On the Hill of Calves and on the grassy flats below, in all the high green corries of the empounding hills, were smaller herds, 100 or 200 strong. From his seat he could count more than 1,500 deer. How many more lay in dead ground, in the vast bay of pastures southwards beyond the high ridge, in high corries and in the hidden recesses of the deep glens, he could not guess, but certainly there would be several hundred hinds in the glens. But here within view, in this mountain sanctuary, were congregated such a head of deer as fell to the lot of few men to see.

It was on those southern heights, comparatively free from peat-hags and rocky outcrop, that the swards of grass and sedge were most luxuriant, with sheep's fescue and the poa grass, the tufted hair-grass and the alpine foxtail, whose blue flower tufts were barbed with yellow antlers earliest in the summer. It was there that the herd of 100 master stags were always to be found, their mighty antlers silhouetted against the skyline at a distance of more than two miles. Day after day, in fine weather, through each succeeding summer, they were to be seen couched on those heights.

No man could term a deer lazy, but certainly this company of big stags enjoyed to the full their summer vacation on the uplands. For three months, if not disturbed, they moved no further than from end to end of these heights—a range of no more than two miles—and just off them into the high corries at either end. Never had the watcher seen one of these masters even as far north as the lochan. Thus the full extent of their summer beat did not exceed 2,500 acres.

Though the hinds were much more mobile, wandering over all the uplands and up onto the 4,000-feet ridges, they normally kept off the master stags' reserve, and the majority of them summered on the illimitable wilderness of high moors and bogs between 2,000 and 3,000 feet, and in the mountain glens, which might be little higher than their wintering glens, though within the hills. The young stags also wandered the uplands, but kept off the high ridges, often going down into the wintering glens at night.

The uplands were mainly a stag reserve. More than three-quarters of the deer that the watcher could see were stags. Twelve hundred stags! One in every ten a master of masters. From how many deer forests, and from how many miles distant had these stags made their way to these traditional summer pastures?—this undulating down-like tundra, seamed with deep watercourses, which were still blocked with solid drifts of snow scores of yards long and five or six feet deep, and shelving gently or steeply up to equally seamed and corrie'd hills.

But for all their numbers, the deer were not happy. Though some were feeding, most were couched in the peat "crumbles", sorely troubled by the flies, of which a swarm of a couple of hundred—the common house-fly, by all appearances—had accompanied the watcher all the way up the stalker's path. Despite an at times cool veering breeze, the swarm remained with him almost continuously throughout the day, concentrated in a cloud around head and face, so that it was almost impossible to eat or drink.

If the deer could not escape this plague at an altitude of 3,000 or 4,000 feet, where could they find refuge? Happily, they were at least spared the additional torments of midges and of clegs and gadflies, which were uncommon visitors to the uplands, for their incessant biting and buzzing threats of bites were maddening enough to stampede deer feeding on the lower hills of the West.

The plague of house-flies was, however, sufficiently irritating to have broken down almost all sex barriers among the deer, and the great herd on the southern heights presented an extraordinary confusion of hinds, calves and stags, with dappled, red-coated calves trotting along beside mighty royals. Even when the deer shifted restlessly from one place to another, they made no attempt to split up into conventional herds.

Many of the older stags, varying in colour from dark red-brown to, in the case of one or two aged beasts, a pale bleached fawn, were couched in the tindery peat lanes and crumbles, heads stretched out on the peat, collie-like, eyes blinking with the flies: while behind them, across the grassy heights, rushed a shimmering grey tidal-bore of heat waves.

One or two of these big fellows had hard antlers clear of velvet, and must therefore have cast their old antlers before the end of March. Though up and down with the flies, they bore the torment more resignedly than the younger stags, who twisted and tossed their heads, rolled over onto their backs on the dry peat, and sprang to their feet again.

Sitting among the crumbles, only 150 yards from them, the watcher was almost, or quite, invisible. Nevertheless his presence was felt. One by one, over a period of fifteen minutes, the nearest stags got up and stretched luxuriously, flexing their hind legs almost horizontally—to begin grazing immediately, of course. Whenever a deer got to its feet, its automatic reaction was to begin feeding. But, although all their movements were leisurely and unalarmed, their grazing course was away from the watcher. Those still seated, got up in their turn as their fellows passed them, and the last to leave trotted off in a bunch.

Among these was a small stag with antlers clean of velvet, who had been enjoying himself bullying one of the masters, a very fat stag. Knowing full well that the master, whose antlers were still tender, would not retaliate, this small stag had deliberately horned him up from his couch again and again. And now, to crown all, as the herd began to climb a steep brae face, with the fat fellow making heavy weather of it, the little stag suddenly turned about and charged the latter in the flank, bowling him over down the slope. He would not have that privilege during the Rut!

To add to the deer's discomfort the nostril-fly was still working, for the tops of the highest hills were this insect's headquarters. The younger hinds were especially troubled, continually breaking into sudden runs or canters, tails stuck straight out, or as straight as their curved tips would allow; and one young hind, thus persecuted, bucked and pranced and swivelled, stiff-legged, snorting and shaking her head and pawing at her nose in the most pathetic manner; while, from time to time, other hinds, grazing on the slopes of one high hill, would suddenly come running down, to splash into the pools below the Hill of Calves and, putting their heads down to the water, spin round and round. Then, after perhaps rolling in a pool, they would climb up to that one remaining snowfield, still clinging to a high scree on the hill, there to wipe their muzzles on the snow, or to couch down and rub their heads on it.

* * * * *

Though the biggest herd was predominantly stags, its extreme north end, low down on the mosses, had in the beginning comprised a group of 100 hinds, with more than forty calves and only a few stags. Most of the hinds were dozing in the sun, though a few were, inevitably, on their feet grazing; while,

in due course, an old girl walked stiffly off to roll
in a soft peat-bank. Her wallowing antics fascinated
a maiden hind standing on the edge of the bank, her
head on one side the better to see; and her curiosity
eventually irritated the old hind so much that she
suddenly jumped out of the bog-hole and lashed out
savagely with her hind hooves at the interloper, who
however, shied away evasively and cantered off in
a fright.

The watcher grinned. What ignorance it was for
Man to set himself up on a pedestal, deeming the
remainder of creation automatons!

Three quarters of an hour after noon a yearling
hind and a calf were both enjoying a long suck from
one mother, and by one o'clock nearly all the hinds
had got up to feed—the nearest within 250 yards of
the watcher—though, as usual, one or another would
sit down to cud every now and again.

The watcher was sitting up against a large rock in
that broken country around the lochan, and gradually
the hinds grazed towards him. As the gap was
narrowed from 250 yards to 100 yards, and then to
fifty yards, and finally one hind with a calf was only
twenty paces distant, his excitement heightened. Was
there to be a repeat of that memorable evening in
the Deep Glen?

Though there was only the lightest of airs, it was
not steady, and anything might happen. Anything,
indeed! Already those silky sensitive ears were
cupped forward as the hind snuffed the air, nostrils
expanded. Even the calf had moved one ear sideways
and then back.

Nothing doing, though: the breeze had veered

again. But the outline of that rock was strange and required closer investigation. The female of the species was ever inquisitive, and none more so than the red deer hind. She came forward tentatively, head and neck almost in one straight line with her back, in her eagerness to extract the minutest particle of scent from that fickle breeze.

No, it was just the same old rock she had known these past ten summers, and yet . . . She retreated a few paces, tried to the right for the wind and then to the left. Still nothing. Forward again, snuffing, staring, nose wrinkling; eyes blinking; head now a little on this side, now a little on that: ears going all ways, now both cupped together, now one forward and one back, now both sticking straight up.

A leap forward and the watcher could have touched that moist black nose.

Perhaps she sensed his tenseness, for she retreated once more with stilted mincing steps, before turning to gaze again. Easy meat, my dear!

But now, another veering puff, a strong one this time. Gone in an instant, true; but he would have to wait for the day when a hind would nibble his fingers. As if struck by a bullet, she gave a great bound and was away . . . leaving the watcher to relax and mop off some of the flies.

The remainder of the hinds now cantered off in bunches; but since only the one hind had got his wind they were not much alarmed, grazing and stopping to suckle their calves as they went; and as one group passed over a knoll into a hollow, so a hind in the rear group would stay on the knoll, looking back, until the leaders had breasted the next knoll.

Then she too would trot off. This was a not uncommon, though by no means regular, practice of hinds on the retreat.

Finally, all the hinds massed on a ridge, for a prolonged gaze, before cantering off once more towards the southern heights, with heads tossing and ears lopping back alternately.

As so often happened, they left behind them two calves, sitting a considerable distance apart among the peat crumbles, unaware of their mothers' departure. One big calf galloped off in the same direction as the herd when the watcher was within fifty paces of it, but the other little fellow, after a scuttering bound almost from his feet, paused irresolute, and then trotted hesitantly up to him. The watcher stretched out his fingers gently, and the calf stretched out its little muzzle to sniff, and then gave a small leap back; but when he walked on, it trotted after him, a pace or two in the rear.

Some stalkers believed that a calf would follow a man if it had not previously followed its mother, but since this calf could already trot strongly it was almost certain that it must have run with its mother for at least a day.

To be followed by a red deer calf was a delightful experience, but as minute followed minute, and the calf still trotted along at heel, the watcher began to feel that one could have too much of a good thing. He could not go stalking over the uplands all day with a calf for company! Already there was a big stag on a knoll some 350 yards distant who had his eye on him, though he did not bother to get up. A stag could hardly expect to see a calf following any-

thing else except a hind! But, whether a hind would
be deceived was another matter. And, indeed, when
five minutes later the watcher was fifty yards nearer
the stag, though almost hidden in dead ground, a
hind did get up and after three minutes' deliberation
took the stag away with her.

The calf had been following him for nearly a mile
now. There was only one thing to do. When near
the stag's knoll—another of those rocky cairns or
kopjes, so characteristic of the uplands—the watcher
made a dash for its far side, and then cautiously
clambered round the cairn. The calf following, had
passed the cairn and was now down-wind of him.
Feeling a little regretful, the watcher slithered down
the cairn's blind side and made a long detour through
the crumbles round the knoll.

Three-quarters of an hour later he sighted the
leading hinds of the calf's herd feeding on the domed
crest of another hill to the south, gradually making
their way down into the Deep Glen.

No matter, the calf's mother would return in the
evening and soon pick up its trail.

*   *   *   *   *

As the afternoon wore on the westerly breeze began
to freshen, though the sun was still very hot, and the
deer began to feed, or fly-run, up the steep slope to
the big stags' heights. They did not, however, feed
directly into the wind, though had they done so they
might have gained some relief from the flies, which
lay behind a deer's head when it walked up-wind.

By this time the watcher was directly behind and
down-wind of the main herd, and was often coming

within a few yards of laggard young stags, dozing
in the sun. At one point he found himself up-wind
of a dozen stags, sitting below him on a broad cornice
of snow, which projected from the lip of the highest
punchbowl corrie at the head of the Deep Glen.
Three big ones among them ran off as he came into
view, but the remainder, together with a further
fifteen hinds and followers feeding on the green slope
beneath, took no notice of, or did not observe, their
departure.

How long would it take scent to reach them? He
lit a cigarette. Five minutes later the whole herd
galloped precipitately over the east ridge of the corrie,
leaving behind, however, one yearling, sitting with
its tail to him on the upper edge of the snow. It was
another five minutes before this one eventually walked
slowly off in the same direction.

When hunting deer the stalkers of his grandfather's
day had often carried lighted peats, whose fragrant
reek, familiar to the forest deer who passed so much
of their life on the low ground, was stronger than a
man's body odour. Tobacco smoke, however, was
not apparently so effective; or had the deer winded
him, rather than the smoke?

That deer did sleep soundly on occasions was
proved by the feat of more than one stalker who had
caught a hind, yes a hind, by hind-leg or ear, when
asleep! Big stags might rest in one place for two
hours, and longer, at a time at midday and in the
late evening. But certainly true sleep was not a
feature of the red deer's life—or of the roe deer's
either, though he recalled a very warm October
afternoon when he had been out with his collies for a

stroll on the moor above the house. In a white shirt
himself, and with the two dogs ranging far ahead, he
had walked down-wind to within forty yards of a buck,
the tips of whose horns could just be seen above a
bank. At that point he had sat down, the dogs puffing
and panting beside him, and a full minute passed,
before the buck pricked up his ears, and was away
with a bound.

Roe deer, though always more timid than red deer,
were not unduly alarmed by Man, when feeding out
on their home moor, not more than a mile or so from
their forest harbourage; but it was a very different
tale when one caught them high up in the hills, as
one sometimes did in the dead of winter, when the
only feeding available was on exposed knolls and steep
faces swept partially bare of snow by high winds.

There had been that December afternoon when
the watcher, out looking for hinds in soft driving snow,
nearly 2,000 feet up on the hill, had surprised a doe
and her two fawns together with a yearling buck,
just in the pride of sprouting his first tiny yellow-
brown dags, a bare inch in length, which projected
from white bosses well forward of his ears. They
were three miles from their home wood, and for
twenty minutes the doe had led the three youngsters,
strung out from thirty to seventy-five yards apart, at
an almost unbroken gallop, now south-west, then
north-west, and finally south-east to and fro and
ultimately down the hill—minute black figures against
the grey-white wilderness of hill; and for all the
watcher knew, they were galloping yet. Only the
most extraordinary alarm would stampede red deer to
that extent.

11

It was a curious fact that the roe, though essentially
woodland deer—less so in the Highlands than elsewhere—possessed much acuter vision than red deer,
and could identify the human figure as immediately
as a mountain sheep. Thus, coming down from the
uplands, one sunny evening early in August, the
watcher had been spotted by a roe-buck at a distance
of half a mile, and it had been a glorious sight to see
that beautiful sandy red-buck, with very long straight
horns, stretched out at full gallop down the green
corrie over the fearfully broken ground with its
hidden rocks, and leaping from bank to bank of the
burns, in his headlong descent from his feeding place
at a height of 2,500 feet. For a red deer to identify
a man at that distance, without the wind in his
favour, would, again, be quite exceptional; and roe
in retreat were indeed often the first to give the alarm
to stags feeding on low moors in winter.

*   *   *   *   *

At five o'clock he was sitting back against his ruck-
sack, legs outstretched, on a breeze-rippled grassy
slope, looking across a deep gully to the steep face of
the southern heights, on the skyline of which were
massed some 250 deer, among them some fifty or
seventy-five of the biggest stags. But while the bulk
of these were gradually feeding over the skyline, a
group of forty stags broke away at right-angles, to
graze along the face of the hill. Though some big stags
were included in this group the leader was a young
stag. Thus were new groupings of deer constituted.
Irritable with the flies, there was some chivying
and biting among the stags, and two reared up per-

fectly straight, slapping with their forelegs, one actually making a jump forward clear of the ground in this upright posture. There was no sparring with antlers of course, none of this small herd having clean antlers, though one of the two boxers did subsequently dig his rival in the rump when the latter was walking in front of him.

Within twenty minutes of breaking away from the main herd, this small group had itself split in two, with all but one of the front portion sitting on the hill, while those in the rear portion marched along the ridge above.

The massed gathering on the ridge had apparently attracted the attention of another large herd, feeding a mile distant on a sweep of upland to the north and up-wind of the watcher, and he was suddenly aware that this herd was streaming down across the upper course of the gully onto his slope and that opposite. Lying on the open hillside, with not even a rock to serve as cover, he could do no more than sit back motionless; but very shortly more than a hundred young stags, with here and there a yearling hind or a hind and her blaring calf, were walking and trotting past him, snatching hasty bites as they went—and a ragged, moulting lot they were, with hardly a big stag among them. Tossing their heads, grunting and "blowing their noses", they passed within twenty yards of him, unwitting. They might just as well have streamed over his outstretched feet. So far as they were concerned he was cloaked in a mantle of in-visibility. The nearest merely glanced at him briefly as they passed, and that was all there was to it. Two indeed, an eight-pointer and a ten-pointer, actually

couched down thirty-five yards up-wind of him, the
latter looking at him curiously as he turned on his
side with binoculars raised.

Later that evening he hoped that he was going to
have the same charmed experience when another
herd of 200 stags, grazing up-wind, suddenly wheeled
round and came galloping straight for him. But to
his disappointment they passed into dead ground
just below him. Had they checked at his morning
scent? It was as difficult to determine the cause of
these sudden panics, as it was to understand the
reasons for those occasional instances when a deer's
nose failed it.

He recalled another July day when at a point 3,000
feet up the bridle-path to the uplands he had looked
back to perceive fourteen stags filing through the
defile from the Red Corrie, some 400 yards below him.
The leading stag, a ten-pointer with the back of his
ears dazzlingly white in the dull light, was highly
suspicious of the path, sniffing at it repeatedly and
looking not only downhill into the wind, but also
uphill, which was unusual. Some young stags behind
him also looked both ways; but, contrary to the
watcher's expectations, there was no shying away
from what ought to have been a fresh scent. Most of
the stags, indeed, grazed for a few moments at the
edge of the path, before feeding hastily down the
slope to the nearest burn, crossing without drinking,
and picking their way up the far slope, where they
settled to feed on the flat above.

The breeze was blowing up the path, conditions
were good for scent lying, and less than an hour had
elapsed, since the watcher had passed that point. It

did not seem possible for the stags to have crossed the path, sniffing its edge on which he had walked, and not have caught some trace of that scent they feared most, and which should have been strong for several hours. Either a deer's nose was not so infallible as supposed, or, conversely, human scent was quickly dispersed by a light wind: just as a hot summer sun after a shower of rain obliterated scent, drawing it up, as it drew the fragrance from the birch leaves and the honey sweetness from the thyme.

*   *   *   *   *

Evening drew on, and still the deer fed into the sunset; and after, when wind-streamered rose-pink bars of cloud and gold-flecked cloudlets yet coloured the northern sky, though westwards all was veiled and sullen, blue-grey range on range, grey-white cloud-layer upon layer, with far below the burnished silver bill-hook of the river snaking through the strath. Already the heat of the day (and the flies) were gone, and it was bitterly cold.

As he retraced his steps across the mosses, bound for the corrie of the snow-buntings, herd after herd of deer, trotting before him, were swallowed up in the concealing dusk; while from all around him sounded the soft mournful whistles of unseen plover— those familiar spirits of the high places.

There were deer everywhere. It was fair to say that on all the 15,000 acres of the uplands there was not one square yard of peat-hag that had not borne the slot of a deer's hoof—here and there the long, narrow, pointed imprint of a hind's hoof, but mainly the broad, rounded and deep slots of stags.

At midnight the silhouettes of feeding deer were still outlined on the 4,000-foot lip of the corrie against the northern sky's dull red glow. So long as there was light the deer would continue to feed—and after that? No man could say, though in these northern regions it was never darker than twilight on a fair night.

The freshening night wind gathered dank clouds from those terrible fanged corries flanking the Glen of the Tainchel, and swept them up to the watcher, lying up against a rock, looking up at the faint worlds of the Plough and the North Star.

For four hours the deer vanished from his ken, until a perceptible lightness began to steal into the corrie, and the faint brown flush of dawn stained a cloud above the screes. Then, when the first ptarmigan "crackled" and the cock snow-bunting began to pipe mournfully from a snowfield high up on one side of the corrie, deer once again grazed over the skyline. Surely they had wandered and fed all night.

Homeward bound, at five o'clock, he saw that, as on the previous day, there were deer everywhere; but at this early hour they were scattered in small herds to every quarter of the compass, from the highest flat downwards. A cross-wind was blowing, and he was continually coming up against these herds, approaching to within fifty yards of one hind with yearling and calf.

It would be a short day on the uplands for them. An eclipse of the sun was due in the afternoon, and already the south wind was strengthening to gale force.

V

THE END OF THE WATCH

BEFORE July was out the early autumn of the uplands had singed the sharp tips of sedge and bent a bright chrome-brown.

In August ephemeral falls of snow dusted the highest ridges, and hoar-frost rimed the grass in the glens.

But the grazing on the uplands remained good, and there was no decline in the numbers of deer feeding on them in good weather to a height of over 4,000 feet. Neither stags nor staggies ever climbed as high as those gritty flats, except when wandering the high ways during the Rut, but from one week to another the watcher would find the same small herd of no more than ten or a dozen hinds, with their calves, up there. These adventurous spirits were 3,000 feet above their wintering glens and eight miles from the nearest.

A few hinds had still to calve, and one or two would not do so until the autumn; but all were now clad in their full summer coats, varying from a lovely chestnut, with peach-coloured rumps, in the case of the fat yeld hinds to a pale fawn in that of the older milk hinds, while the calves themselves were losing their spots and would soon resemble the maiden hinds in colour, though their coats would be soft and woolly throughout the winter.

After being four months in velvet, most of the big stags and some of the younger ones had succeeded, after a couple of weeks' scraping, and even chewing, in getting rid of this velvet, which for some days had been hanging in strips from their antlers—an oddity exaggerated by the addition of long pennons of moss streaming in the wind as they trotted or cantered: for these upland stags had, perforce, to clean their antlers against rocks covered with cushion-moss or on hummocks of fringe-moss, and six or seven could be observed engaged in so doing at one time, while their fellows couched in the sun or fed peacefully.

This was a sad sight, for that thick leaden-coloured velvety pile had enhanced the magnificence and softened the contours of those splendid antlers, and the ivory-white of newly clean antlers soon darkened. Not for these upland stags the pleasure of being able to rake their antlers through the tough stems of old heather, which was much the most efficient remover of this now dead and shrivelled encumbrance.

Though hundreds of deer were still thronging the uplands at the end of August, there were signs that their short season in their mountain sanctuary was drawing to a close. They were often difficult to find at this season of dispersal, especially on stormy days, when the wind sweeping across the uplands streamed down into the mountain glens, whipping up white wave-caps on the blue-black lochs. The sawn-off head of such a glen would, however, be sheltered and sunny, and often provided a haven of refuge for one small herd of ten or twenty hinds. Bigger herds of upwards of a hundred hinds might already be visiting the upper reaches of such traditional rutting places as the Red Corrie, or even be down on the floor of the Glen of Crags—now a glorious wild garden of dark-green thickets of juniper, grassy glades and, above all, purple tracts of heather which, as the dark evening shadows lengthened across the moors, were thrown into high relief against the black-green canopy of pines, so that for mile after mile the glen was a smouldering purple, a rich cloak of colour enveloping the watcher with an almost physical warmth, such was its contrast to the driving wind and dank cloud on the uplands above.

Moreover, if one herd of fifty-five big stags might still be found grazing on the green walls of the Deep Glen's punchbowl corries, some of the biggest members of the herd of masters on the southern heights had nevertheless disappeared, and so forward in condition were they that once or twice the watcher heard distant roaring—a muffled bellowing at this early date; while those that remained were unusually active, bucking and prancing and digging one another, not altogether playfully, in ribs or buttocks, blooding the bone-white tines of their now clean, brown antlers; or galloping after one another aimlessly—when rain threatened, some stalkers believed.

Nor was this unwonted wildness a matter of behaviour only. A certain savagery was noticeable in their aspect, with the growth of their heavy winter manes and the appearance of dark furrows down their faces, scored by the "tears" from the glands below their eyes.

The older stags had memories, no doubt, of past rutting seasons to excite them and urge them to wander; and there were occasions when, restless with the physical change in their bodies, whole herds might be infected by this compelling urge to wander, and a herd of as many as fifty stags might

travel fifty miles across-country in as many hours,
in these pre-rutting days. One or two might even
be among the glen hinds, though not actually rutting,
before the first week in September was out. That
was a phenomenon of the red deer's mating. One
September day a herd of thirteen stags might be
feeding between two herds of hinds, apparently
indifferent to them. The next day one or more of
these same stags might be actively rutting.

But what drew the hinds down to the glens? A
hind was only interested in stags for a few hours
during the whole course of the Rut, and while the
grazing might be going back on the uplands, and
there might be a sharp frost on a night here and
there, September days were often the warmest and
finest of the summer. Moreover some hinds might
not come into season until January or February.

Such traditional rutting places as the Eagles' Glen
had not been entirely deserted during the summer
months, for on some evenings as many as a hundred
hinds had ventured down from the 3,000-feet tops,
to graze on the marshy flat on the floor of the glen;
while, if the majority of the wintering herd of a hundred stags had left the glen heights for the uplands
as soon as their antlers were well grown in the early
summer, a dozen or so of the younger beasts had
summered at home.

It was on a day in mid-September that the watcher
repaired once again to that famous rutting glen. A
dry spell had been broken two days earlier by equi-
noctial gales and heavy rains, and a squally west
wind was blowing, with intermittent heavy showers,
though good sunny intervals. White-winged goos-

anders sped up-river before him, and a young
cormorant was a storm-driven stranger to the white
crested waters of the loch, while the ancient birch
wood, now high-lighted with the orange and coral
globes of rowan berries, was full of the stony "chacking"
and throaty trills of mountain-ousels whirling from
tree to tree in wild flight.

He was yet four miles distant when he perceived
that the deer were down in strength. Clustered
dots, hinds of course, speckled the sunlit velvety
green of the Rowan Corrie; while nearer at hand a
tiny "frieze" of hinds were grazing into the wind
along the ridge of the great Hill of Roaring Stags;
and, yes, there was one small stag with them.

Though 800 feet above the glen the hinds were
easily detectable as such by their antelope-like
figures and, at that distance, small heads and humped
bodies. Indeed at any range, when their brown-grey
faces and necks, particularly dark-brown on the nape,
were almost hidden against the brown-green heather,
and their long lop-eared silhouettes were lost, hinds
were surprisingly gazelle-like with their yellow bodies
and long legs, and in their delicate graceful movements.

It was one o'clock before he had reached the foot
of the Rowan Corrie, which rose steeply from the
loch side, culminating in the usual amphitheatre
immediately below the crags, a thousand feet above
the loch. It would not, he saw, be possible to approach
closer than 400 yards to the main body of the herd,
which he estimated to number seventy-five hinds
and followers—no stags.

It was most difficult to make an accurate tally of

an undisturbed herd of hinds, especially when one
was looking into the sun. There were always some
hinds up and some down, and though the grass in
this particular corrie was not long, the calves were
more or less swallowed up in it, while an occasional
long-handled Y might in fact betoken the presence
of half a dozen hinds couched within a few yards
of each other; for only the heads could be seen of
most of those at rest, sprawled about in the comfortably ungainly attitudes of kangaroos—which they
somewhat resembled, with their grey cheeks and
sandy coats, their white underparts and immensely
long hind legs. Had the watcher not been aware
that there was no bogwood in this part of the corrie,
he would have mistaken those dark heads and ears
for broken snags sticking up from the peat; and
when the sun shone forth strongly again after a
heavy shower, quite unsuspected hinds were revealed,
when here and there sudden puffs of mist dissolved
over the sparkling green, as they rose and shook
themselves. Your deer scorned to turn their backs
on driving rain, continuing to feed head to wind or
sit orientated to all quarters of the compass.

Little by little the watcher crawled up behind a
series of convenient heather knolls, squelching through
the peat and sphagnum moss; and despite a number
of cackling explosions from bursting grouse, of which
the deer took no notice, had approached, after half
an hour, to within 200 yards of the nearest outlying
hind, who had two good-sized calves with her.

So rarely were twins born to a red deer that one
could always safely assume that when a hind was
seen with two calves, one was not her own. So now,

when one calf butted the other to its feet, the hind chased the offender away, slapping at it with her forefeet. As it was in good condition it was probably not an orphan, but had merely strayed from its mother, feeding elsewhere in the corrie.

At two o'clock the hind lay down, as did the two calves, her own close beside her, the other twenty yards away. For twenty-five minutes they cudded peacefully. Then, a sudden volley of strong veering gusts brought the hind to her feet, and she stamped her right foot seven times at intervals, but indecisively, almost as if pained with rheumatism—a curious antic, denoting disquiet and bewilderment, and one common to the two-year-old staggie, when his mother chased him roughly away before she calved.

After looking in various directions, both down and up the corrie, the hind then stretched, walked slowly as far as the stray calf, which was also on its feet, and finally turned to face the watcher, the long hairs fringing the lower edge of her ears transparent against the strong sun shining behind her. Then, returning to her own calf, she met its nose with hers, ears laid half back playfully, and the calf sucked for half a minute, while she stood cudding impassively. Then she brought her leg forward sharply and walked on impatiently before the calf had drunk its fill. Hinds were not very elegant at this season, with swollen stomachs bulging from a summer's good feeding—still less elegant when they stood, pot-bellies sagging, tails stuck out, while their calves sucked.

During his stalk the watcher had not entirely escaped notice, for he had aroused the suspicions of the highest-placed hind in the herd, 600 feet above him and some 400 yards distant. For forty-five minutes, without a second's break, or the slightest movement of her forefeet, raised on a little mound in front of her, this hind had stood looking down at him, or at any rate in his direction. He could not recall any comparable period of unbroken concentration by a deer; and when at the end of that long spell, in which none of her companions had joined, she turned away to graze, it was to do so for a few minutes only. Then she couched down and resumed her watch, while chewing the cud; and when he finally got up, after a lie of one and a half hours, she spotted him immediately.

The herd, six or seven mountain sheep among them, had now been feeding down and across the amphitheatre for at least four hours. Despite a number of heavy rainstorms they had grazed industriously on the grass among the heather, travelling very slowly, often spending several minutes feeding round and about one particularly choice spot. Completely at peace, they had rarely bothered to look up, though when one moved round a rock or knoll, she was likely to point her ears forward and stand for a second or two, forelegs drawn up together, before walking on to a fresh patch.

When the watcher moved up the pony-path, climbing parallel with the corrie, the herd gradually bunched together in a sweeping dark-brown crescent in the womb of the amphitheatre, which was now in shade, with the sun behind the horn of the hill. And there were not 75 hinds and followers, but, in fact, 135. With the sun directly in his eyes, giving a misty field of view through binoculars, he had overlooked nearly half the herd. Year after year this herd of between 135 and 170 hinds and followers frequented this corrie in the autumn.

It was only on moving that he became aware that there were more deer on his side of the glen, and that a herd of twenty hinds included three fair-sized stags. So there they were, then—the first big stags he had seen in a rutting glen this autumn.

But they were not yet rutting. They were fat and "out of training." The biggest of them puffed and panted, as he breasted the steep siding with the motion of a horse pulling a heavy load characteristic of the climbing stag.

Such a stag if killed would be found to have solid pads of fat, two or three inches thick, on his rump, though his neck would hardly have begun to thicken.

Nor was the big stag at home in this glen. He was very anxious to get out of the dangerous confines of this cleft in the hills, leading the way in a hurry along a path under the crags, followed by the second biggest stag, with the hinds tailing off more leisurely.

*　　*　　*　　*　　*

At the head of the glen, at a height of 2,500 feet, where ptarmigan and grouse met and a twittering pack of young golden plover flashed white and gold in the wet glare of the westering sun, as they circled and banked over the mosses, the hills fell away on their reverse side to an undulating plain of moors, backed by more endless ranges of hills. Here, at the water-

shed, was another big herd of some 200 hinds, and
with them six or ten big stags. They, too, were shy
and trotted away immediately.

This great plain was a favourite wintering ground
for hinds, with no township within six miles. Across
it, before a blizzard, the watcher had observed with
awe the migration of hundreds and hundreds of hinds
walking, not trotting or cantering, but walking
steadily, one behind another, down to the shelter of
the glens and innumerable watercourses. Two
thousand deer he had counted that day, and hardly
a big stag among them.

What man knew the secret winter life of these
out-bye herds?

Evening was drawing in when the watcher found
himself on the immense tableland forming the
"crest" of the Hill of Roaring Stags: a shelving flat
of heather and bog a mile across from side to side.
Through the misty curtains of driving showers he
saw that the hill was alive with deer. 500 yards
below him twenty hinds and a small stag still in
velvet were running from his wind. Before him
straggled a big herd of a hundred or more hinds,
and with them five really big stags, and an eagle
flapping low over their heads. Twenty more hinds
and four big stags were moving up to join them,
while on that face of the hill falling steeply to the
rutting ravine another forty or fifty hinds were
feeding, with a further ten already down on the
floor of the glen. In the rain-washed shadow,
illumined by the last of the light, their colouring was
rich, almost salmon-pink; and then, as he slithered
down the steep sidings into the glen, all were lost in

another rainstorm against the dull purple hills of fading heather.

In all, then, he had seen well over 500 hinds and between fifteen and twenty big stags. There were no indications that the Rut had begun, but the clans were gathering.

*　　*　　*　　*　　*

A week later, after three or four sunny, frosty days, the Rut had advanced a stage further. True, there were still very few stags in the Eagles' Glen, and none had been heard roaring, but many of the hinds were spaced evenly in small groups along the sidings on either side of the ravines, as they would be during the actual Rut—here three, there eight, there ten; and what was that? Two or three hinds sitting on the crest of a hill? That was unusual. Only stags did that.

The watcher crossed the burn to investigate, but when halfway up the opposite hill it struck him that there was something familiar about that sardonic figure sitting there impassively, watching him all the way up the path until he was almost abreast and 200 yards distant.

Only then did He rise. Yes, it was He, of course— a great wolf of a thick-maned hummel, shaggier and a darker brown than the tawny hind and calf feeding hardby. Trust a hummel to be early among the hinds! And he had been visiting his peat wallow, too. Black lumps of peat plastered his sides.

He was indeed the only mature stag that the watcher saw all day.

The hind had much difficulty in assessing the

12

watcher's danger value, but finally she barked once or twice and led the way over the top, followed somewhat sleepily by her lord, after he had stretched.

A strong south wind had now got up, driving the cloud down on the high moors, and the watcher soon found himself groping his way through mist with visibility down to fifty yards. As the mist eddied, so small groups of hinds were revealed standing watching him, and then they were swallowed up in the mist again.

A grim, sullen place, this Eagles' Glen, on such an evening.

*   *   *   *   *

This was an autumn of persistent strong south winds.

Day after day the tops above 2,000 feet were wrapped in cloud, while a gloomy haze obscured the glens.

The deer calves could have wished for no better weather, for hard weather in the fall affected the hinds' flow of milk, so that many calves died. Milk was essential until the end of the year. After that some hinds might go dry without their calves suffering in a moderately open winter. But for this extraordinarily prolonged lactation of the hinds, the red deer could not have survived the rigours of winter in these mid-Highland forests.

Nature usually managed to strike a balance with her seasons. It had been a bad calving season after the long winter, but now a mild autumn would make it possible for a good proportion of calves to win through the winter.

The effect of this phenomenal weather on the course of the Rut was most interesting. Though all but a few scores of deer, and these nearly all hinds with a few small stags, had abandoned the uplands by the middle of September, not a stag was to be heard roaring in the Eagles' Glen until the second day of October; and when the watcher visited the glen again at mid-month, it was to enter a strangely silent and empty forest.

It was almost noon before he saw his first stag—a six-pointer of no great size couched quietly on a hill face, with his harem of sixteen hinds and followers grazing nearby.

600 yards further up the ravine was another herd of hinds, but no stag; and a few hundred yards further still a hind with a calf, and a stag running from them over the crest of the ridge. A running stag promised action: so the watcher sat down on the opposite side of the gorge to await events, and very shortly perceived that the stag was climbing steadily up to a higher ridge towards a hind and her calf, who stood looking down upon him apprehensively. As he approached them the hind suddenly leaped about and cantered up the hill. The stag gave chase and eventually turned her beneath an overhanging crag. He was angry now, and standing no nonsense, charged her savagely down the hill with a prod in the rump, and they disappeared into dead ground.

In the meantime four hinds had picked their way over the crest immediately above the watcher, and later a long moo sounded from the head of the defile. At this, the hinds looked up, and almost at once the stag, a big seven-pointer, re-appeared, driving the hind and her calf before him. Three times he stood at gaze and roared, or rather bellowed, for there was little savagery in his challenge, jetting clouds of vapour into the fitful gleams of sun—an exhalation from excitement perhaps, rather than from his exertions, though he was certainly fat. Then he would pace along the ridge after his prize, to join the other hinds, the fringe of his mane jagged against the skyline.

On rejoining his harem of ten, who were grazing along and below the crest, he walked slowly around them, head stretched out and lifted a little, tongue licking nostrils; but the hinds would have nothing to do with these tongue-flickering advances, making little runs out of his way, as did the calves, looking backward at him coming. From time to time he would stand motionless for short intervals, occasionally lowering his muzzle to the ground, as if to listen more closely for a roar or perhaps pick up the vibrations of hooves. Once he plunged into a burn, to emerge dripping on the other side. In forty minutes he roared only seven times without menace, lifting his head anew for each series of from one to three cater-wauls terminating the roar. But not once did he get a reply. Life was very dull. There was no rival to hear him. The weather was so mild that the majority of the stags and a great many of the hinds were not coming down to the rutting glens.

One fact was clear. It was interpreting the procedure of the Rut too rigidly to make it a point that the stags followed the hinds down to the latter's wintering glens for this purpose. In normal autumns, with a big drop in the night temperatures in October, yes; but in a mild, open autumn, no. In these circumstances only a few of the hinds came down to feed below 2,500 feet, and the wintering glens were almost devoid of deer. Furthermore, such weather conditions did not stimulate the stags as did those of a normal mountain autumn, with its hard frosts at night and crisp sunny days. This would be a year when the majority of the calves would be sired by young stags coming in late to the hinds at the approach of winter. It was even possible that many hinds would not be mated, and that there would be few calves on the uplands the following summer.

*   *   *   *   *

And so it was that when at last a typical autumn day dawned, with dense fog in the strath early, and a summer sun all day, and the watcher hastened through the pinewoods, bound for the highest mountain in his forest, it was to find the stags wailing and snarling in the very highest corries, and solitary bachelors wandering disconsolately, with frustrated roaring, across one of their main highways over the mountain massif at a height of almost 4,000 feet.

For the last time he looked out over these mountain pastures of his deer, and beyond them for upwards of one hundred miles.

He had come to them as a young man. On them he had spent much of his strength. A fitting sanctuary for the deer, yes; but a hard country for a man. There was none harder in Britain.

Yet their lure would always call him. Strath

bound, a restless urge would seize him, as it possessed the captive bird, when it heard the call-notes of its migrant fellows passing north, and beat its caged wings.

His eyes roved over the old familiar scene—the sterile summit dome of gravel wastes and chaotic fields of boulder-slabs; the crumbling black crags and grey-pink screes of the wild and gloomy ravines; the immense green punchbowl corries, cradling shimmering black tarns; the long waterslides, falling precipitously between sentinel cheese-ring stacks, to the black rocks and molten sands of abyssal lochs; and those brindled tawny, grey and yellow-green uplands, summer playground of the red deer calves.

And, in microcosm, diminutive yellow leaves of dwarf willow; fire-tinted dwarf blaeberry; thick carpets of grey-green fringe-moss, spangled with reindeer moss and brightly painted with green mats of crowberry, with here and there trailing clumps of purple-red azalea still bearing a few pink starlets. . . .

A softly clucking pack of fifty ptarmigan rose from the grey jumble of boulders as a flight of white doves against the blue sky. An arctic wind was freshening. It was time to say good-bye and go down into the long corrie, where a big stag watched his harem of forty hinds; down to the evening stillness of the glen and the cold silvered loch, stained saffron at its fringes by the westering sun; leaving behind those tawny slopes and black crags, sharp in silhouette against the pale sky.

Time to go home through the wooded glen: a roofless abbey, in the twilight, hung with tarnished gold, black, umber and dark brown tapestries of smouldering birches, sullen and oppressive, yet rich and warm, and lit by startling flames of yellow, green and vivid chrome, where cherries, tremulous aspens and groves of poplars towered above the sombre bronze canopy.

*   *   *   *   *

The watch was ended.

HUNCOAT	9 . 72
BAXENDEN	7 . 73
BROAD OAK	
HILL TOP	7 74